BONITA HUSSEY

What's for Supper?

Home-cooked meals from
Bonita's Kitchen to yours

BOULDER
BOOKS

Library and Archives Canada Cataloguing in Publication

Title: What's for supper? : home-cooked meals from Bonita's Kitchen to yours / Bonita Hussey.
Other titles: What is for supper?
Names: Hussey, Bonita 1965- author.
Identifiers: Canadiana 20250174545 | ISBN 9781998220250 (softcover)
Subjects: LCSH: Cooking, Canadian—Newfoundland and Labrador style. | LCSH: Cooking—Newfoundland and Labrador. | LCGFT: Cookbooks.
Classification: LCC TX715.6 .H865 2025 | DDC 641.59718 [illegible]dc23

Published by Boulder Books
Portugal Cove-St. Philip's, Newfoundland and Labrador
www.boulderbooks.ca

Design and layout: Todd Manning
Front cover design: Tanya Montini
Editor: Stephanie Porter
Copy editor: Iona Bulgin
Cover photo: Laura Hussey

Printed in China

We acknowledge the financial support of the Government of Newfoundland and Labrador through the Department of Tourism, Culture and Recreation.

Newfoundland Labrador

Funded by the Government of Canada | Financé par le gouvernement du Canada | Canada

To my mother, Alice Coombs—
friend, taste tester, role model,
and one of my biggest fans.

Bonita's
Kitchen

CONTENTS

Casseroles

Pastries

Salads

Seafood

Entrées

Bonita with her mom's wood stove.

INTRODUCTION

Why did I call my third cookbook *What's for Supper*?

Growing up in the mid-1960s in Newfoundland and Labrador, life was very different from what it is today. There were no iPhones, computers, or electronic games to play.

We spent our days outside, playing in the garden or sneaking down to the ocean to explore the flat rocks. Sometimes we'd venture up into the hills, searching for caves and pretending to be shopkeepers, selling groceries and such. Our family's home was on the ocean's edge, and while my parents didn't allow us to go near the water unless they were with us, we often snuck down anyway, trying not to get caught.

After a full day of playing with friends in our neighbourhood, we'd come home starving. We'd burst into the house and call out to our moms, "WHAT'S FOR SUPPER?"

It wasn't always our favourite meal, but it was always good. Mom would have freshly baked bread with every meal, and sometimes there'd be a nice dessert or pudding—even though times were tough, and food wasn't always plentiful. Dad grew organic vegetables, while Mom made most of the meals, along with bread, cakes, pickles, jams, and jellies. Dad, having learned to cook while working away on the mainland, would often whip up meals that he called "rough grub"—food made from scratch with simple ingredients from our home or garden.

I wanted this cookbook to reflect those days, with food that's easy to make, using simple ingredients that you likely already have at home, in your garden, or from the local store or farmer's market. So many wonderful childhood memories revolve around food, reminding us of family and all the moments shared through making and eating meals together.

This new cookbook isn't just about traditional recipes—it's about affordable, easy-to-make dishes that we've shared on our YouTube channel and website and through requests from friends, family, and viewers. I believe there's something here for everyone, and all the recipes are tried and true.

Each recipe in this book has a corresponding video. Simply visit BonitasKitchen.com, search by recipe name, and follow along with me as you cook. How wonderful is that? And if you have any questions or need to substitute an ingredient, just send me a message—I'd be happy to help!

RECIPE NOTES AND CONVERSIONS

CONVERSION TABLES

The recipes in this book give measurements in cups, tablespoons, ounces, and inches. Temperatures are given in Fahrenheit, still the most popular scale for the majority of North American cooks. Those who prefer to work in millilitres, centimetres, or Celsius, may refer to these conversion tables.

MEASUREMENT EQUIVALENTS

(rounded off for ease of use)

Volume/Weight	Pan Size	Oven Temperature	
		Fahrenheit	Celsius
1 tsp = 5 ml	8 inch × 8 inch = 20 cm × 20 cm	300°	145°
1 tbsp = 15 ml	9 inch x 9 inch = 23 cm x 23 cm	325°	160°
¼ cup = 60 ml	9 inch x 11 inch = 23 cm x 32 cm	350°	175°
⅓ cup = 85 ml	4 inch × 8 inch = 10 cm x 20 cm	375°	190°
½ cup = 125 ml	5 inch × 9 inch = 13 cm x 23 cm	400°	200°
1 cup = 250 ml		450°	230°
4 cups = 1 litre			
1 pound = 450 grams			

LIQUID INGREDIENTS

Use a liquid measuring cup with a pouring spout.

Place cup on a level surface and check at eye level.

For smaller amounts of liquid (1 tbsp or less), fill a measuring spoon to the top without allowing the liquid to spill over.

DRY INGREDIENTS

Lightly spoon ingredients into a dry measuring cup or spoon and level any excess with the flat side of a knife or spatula.

When measuring flour, never pack down, shake or tap the cup before levelling.

When measuring brown sugar or shortening, firmly press the ingredient into the cup before levelling off.

SPECIFIC INGREDIENTS

Sugar: unless stated otherwise, sugar is white granulated.

Evaporated milk: can be standard or 2%, generally purchased in a can. Fresh milk or milk alternative (soy, almond, oat, etc.) may be substituted, though this may slightly affect the flavour.

Milk: I usually use whole milk; any fresh milk or alternative may be used, but this may affect the flavour slightly.

Butter: unless otherwise noted, use unsalted butter. If using salted butter, reduce the salt in the recipe and/or season to taste. Substitute margarine if preferred.

Juice: lemon, lime, and other juices are always best freshly squeezed. Bottled juices may be substituted.

Cream cheese: use full-fat or light.

Sour cream: use full-fat or light.

Pepper: black pepper is listed in most recipes that use pepper; freshly ground is always best. Substitute white pepper if preferred.

A FEW HELPFUL DEFINITIONS

BLANCH: to partially cook in boiling water or steam; also used to loosen skins from tomatoes, peaches, and almonds.

BRAISE: to cook meats slowly in a tightly covered pan using a small amount of liquid.

CUBE: to cut into uniform pieces, usually ½-inch cubes.

DICE: to cut into uniform pieces, usually ⅛- to ¼-inch cubes.

DEGLAZE: to add liquid such as water, wine, or both to a skillet after it has been used to cook meat; also used to create sauce.

FOLD: combine a light mixture, such as beaten egg whites, with a heavy mixture, such as cake batter, without the loss of air. Heavy ingredients are folded directly into the centre of the light ingredients with a spatula and pulled toward the edge of the bowl.

MINCE: to chop food into tiny, irregular pieces.

POACH: to cook food by partially or completely submerging it in a boiling liquid.

PURÉE: to convert a solid into a liquid or heavy paste using a blender or food processor; also refers to the resulting mixture.

Apple butter

Jams, Pickles, and Sauces

Growing up, Mom would always have different homemade jams on the table, ready to serve with the white bread that accompanied every meal.

And, of course, there was always a cup of strong, hot tea steeped in a teapot on the wood stove.

We'd also find bottles of pickles on the table, each with a fork or spoon in it, because, in a big family, not everyone liked the same pickles. My favourites were pickled beets and mustard pickles.

If the meal called for it, Mom would serve a sauce, and her mustard sauce is one I still love making and sharing at our table.

APPLE BUTTER

7 lb apples of choice

2½ cups white sugar

1¼ cups apple cider vinegar

2½ cups water

½ tsp sea salt

2 tbsp fresh or bottled lemon juice

½ to 1 tsp ground cinnamon

½ tsp ground allspice

½ tsp ground ginger

¼ tsp ground cloves

4 x 500 ml or 8 x 250 ml Mason jars

Wash the apples thoroughly and cut off any bruised areas. Cut the apples into wedges, including the skin and cores as this will contribute pectin.

Place the apples, water, vinegar, and salt in a stockpot with a lid and bring to a boil on a medium heat. Reduce the heat to low and simmer for 10 to 15 minutes, until the apples have softened and broken apart.

Using a potato ricer or sieve and spatula, press the cooked applesauce through it into a bowl, leaving the stems, peels, and seeds behind. Return the applesauce (including the juice) to the stockpot. Add the sugar, spices, and lemon juice, and boil on a low to medium heat, stirring occasionally.

Keep stirring until the mixture is thick and smooth. This can take 1 to 2 hours. Taste the sauce after 1 hour and add more sugar, if needed. The colour will darken slightly as the applesauce thickens. Make sure that it does not burn or stick to the bottom of the stockpot.

To check if the butter is ready, scoop a small amount onto a cold plate. If it sets to your liking, it is ready to bottle; if it does not, cook for a few more minutes.

Sterilize four 500- or eight 250-millilitre Mason jars. Follow the sterilization and canning procedures outlined on page 3 to preserve the apple butter. The butter may also be frozen in containers or vacuum-sealed bags.

Bonita's notes

Apple butter can be frozen for up to 6 months. After a bottle of apple butter has been opened, refrigerate it and eat within a few weeks.

STERILIZATION AND CANNING PROCEDURES

Sterilization

1. Fill a large stockpot about one-quarter full with water.
2. Bring the water to a boil, place the Mason jars inside, and cover.
3. Boil for about 15 to 20 minutes and then remove the bottles and place them upside down on paper towels or a cloth.

Canning

1. When the food items are cooked and ready to place in the bottles, scoop or pour hot liquid or food into the jars, leaving ½ inch of air space at the top.
2. Clean around the tops of the jars to remove any food or liquid.
3. Place the lids and rings on the jars and tighten the rings finger-tight.
4. Place the filled jars back in the hot water bath and boil for another 5 minutes with the cover on the stockpot.
5. Remove the jars from the water and cool to room temperature.

Ensure that the cooled jars are sealed. Touch the lid gently with your finger to ensure that it is depressed. Label and date the jars and store in a cool, dark place.

APPLE PICKLES

6 apples of choice, peeled and diced

6 onions, diced

1 cup white vinegar

1½ cups canned diced tomatoes

1 tbsp pickling spice in cheesecloth or tea steeper

½ cup brown sugar

3 bay leaves (optional)

6 to 8 x 250 ml Mason jars

Combine all ingredients in a medium saucepan. Place on a medium heat and boil 20 to 30 minutes, until the apples and onions start to soften and the mixture reaches the desired texture.

Taste and add more sugar, if desired.

Pour into hot, sterilized Mason jars and follow the procedure on page 3.

Bonita's notes

Purchase ready-made pickling spice or make your own using some or all of these ingredients, to taste: mustard seed, coriander, bay leaves, dill seed, fenugreek, cinnamon, ginger, allspice, red pepper, black pepper, and cloves.

BREAD AND BUTTER PICKLES

8 cups thinly sliced cucumbers

8 cups thinly sliced onions

2 tbsp sea salt

2 cups white vinegar

1½ to 2 cups white sugar (to taste)

1 tsp celery seeds

2 tbsp yellow mustard

1 tbsp yellow mustard seeds

1 tsp turmeric

½ tsp white pepper

2 bay leaves and pickling spice, tied in a piece of cheesecloth

4 to 5 cups ice cubes to cover

8 x 250 ml Mason jars

Place the cucumbers, onions, and salt in a large stockpot. Cover with the ice cubes and let stand for 2 to 3 hours. Add more ice if required to keep the bowl cold.

Combine the vinegar, sugar, celery seeds, mustard, mustard seeds, turmeric, and pepper in another stockpot. Place on a medium heat, bring quickly to a boil and boil for 10 minutes.

Drain the water from the cucumbers and onions, then add them to the vinegar mixture. Bring to a boil, then immediately remove from the heat.

Follow the sterilization and canning procedures outlined on page 3.

Bonita's notes

Celery seed substitutions: 1 teaspoon celery seed equals 2 tablespoons minced celery tops. You may also use celery salt, which is a combination of ground celery seeds and salt, but reduce the amount of sea salt you use in the brine.

BREAD
BUTTER

MOTHER'S MUSTARD SAUCE

⅓ cup dry mustard

2 tsp all-purpose flour

1 cup brown sugar

1 beef bouillon cube

⅓ cup vinegar of choice

3 large eggs

Mix the dry ingredients in a bowl. Crack the eggs in another bowl, whisk well with the vinegar, and add to the dry ingredients. Use a beater or hand whisk to combine thoroughly.

Cook the sauce in a double boiler until thick. You may also cook it in the microwave, stirring every 30 seconds for about 6 minutes.

Pour into a 500-millilitre Mason jar for storage. Add warm water to thin out the mustard if it is too thick.

Serve hot or cold. This will last for months in the refrigerator.

Bonita's notes

Use any vinegar in this recipe. My go-tos are apple cider vinegar or, for a tangier mustard, malt vinegar.
Thank you to my friend Jennifer Leigh Hill for sharing her mom's recipe. Jennifer always cooks her mustard sauce in a microwave. She recently made a batch with rice wine vinegar and says that it resulted in a much different, but pleasant, flavour.

Orange marmalade

ORANGE MARMALADE

5 navel oranges, sliced, tips and stones removed

3 lemons, sliced, tips and stones removed

12 cups cold water

1 cup white sugar for each 1 cup of fruit mixture

8 x 125 ml Mason jars

Place the sliced oranges, lemons, and water in a large stockpot with a lid. Cover and let it stand overnight at room temperature.

Next day, bring the fruit and water to a boil and simmer until the fruit is tender, stirring occasionally. This may take 40 minutes or more. Remove from the heat and allow the mixture to come to room temperature.

Strain the fruit, reserving the juice. Measure the fruit and return it to the stockpot. Add 1 cup sugar for each 1 cup of fruit. Add 2 cups reserved juice; discard the remaining juice or use in another recipe.

Boil until the mixture starts to jell (about 218°F to 220°F on a candy thermometer), stirring occasionally. This may take 40 to 60 minutes. Scoop any foam from the top of the liquid and discard.

If you do not have a candy thermometer, drop a teaspoonful of marmalade onto a cold plate. If it sets to your preference, it is ready to process. If it is still too runny, cook a few minutes more and test again.

Follow the sterilizing and canning procedures on page 3.

Photos on previous page

Bonita's notes

Use navel oranges for best results.

PARTRIDGEBERRY PICKLES

4 cups partridgeberries

4 cups white onions, chopped

1½ cups white sugar

½ cup white vinegar

1 tsp sea salt

½ tsp ground cinnamon

½ tsp ground allspice

¼ tsp ground cloves

¼ tsp black pepper

8 x 250 ml Mason jars

Combine all the ingredients in a large saucepan. Bring to a boil on a medium heat and simmer for about 1 hour.

While the mixture is cooking, prepare eight 250-millilitre Mason jars. Follow the sterilization and canning procedures on page 3. Make sure that the jars are hot when you pour or scoop in the pickles, and leave a ½-inch space at the top of each.

Photos on next pages

Bonita's notes

Fresh or frozen partridgeberries may be used in this recipe. You may substitute red onion for the white onion.

Partridgeberry pickles

PICKLED BEETS

3 lb medium beets

1 tsp sea salt

1 cup white vinegar

1 cup brown sugar

6 x 500 ml prepared Mason jars (see sterilizing procedure page 3)

Wash the beets and place them in a stockpot. Cover with water and add the salt. Boil until the beets are tender.

Drain the beets, reserving the liquid.

Wearing rubber gloves, peel each beet by running a hand over its surface—the peel should slide off easily. Slice the beets (cut smaller, if desired) and place in the jars, leaving 1 inch of space from the rim.

Combine the vinegar, 2 cups beet liquid, and the sugar in a saucepan. Bring to a boil and simmer for 5 minutes.

Pour the hot liquid into the jars, ensuring that the beets are completely covered. Follow the sealing procedure on page 3.

Let the beets sit at room temperature for a few days before eating. Store unopened in a cold pantry; refrigerate after opening.

Bonita's notes

Using the cooking liquid instead of water keeps the beets a darker colour. The secret ingredient is the brown sugar–but you can use all white sugar if you prefer.

BERNARDIN

PICKLED EGGS

12 large eggs

1½ cups white vinegar

1 cup water

½ medium onion, sliced

1 celery stalk, chopped

pinch of sea salt

1 tsp pickling spice

2 bay leaves

½ tsp white sugar

2 x 500 ml prepared Mason jars (see sterilizing procedure page 3)

Place the eggs in a large saucepan. Cover with the water and boil for about 15 minutes until they are hard-boiled. Drain and place the eggs in a bowl of cold water.

Place the rest of the ingredients in a medium saucepan. Bring to a boil and then remove from the heat.

Peel the eggs and place them in the jars and top with the hot vinegar mixture. Divide the onions, celery, and spices between the two jars. Dry the rims and cap each jar, making sure that each is sealed. Cool to room temperature.

Refrigerate after opening.

PICKLED WIENERS

12 large hot dog wieners

1½ cups white vinegar

1 cup water

½ medium onion, sliced

pinch of sea salt

1 tsp pickling spice

2 bay leaves

½ tsp white sugar

2 x 500 ml prepared Mason jars (see sterilizing procedure page 3)

Place the wieners in a large saucepan. Cover with the water and boil for 15 minutes or until cooked.

Follow the same procedure as for the pickled eggs above. Cut the wieners as desired. (Note: there is no celery in this recipe.)

Bonita's notes

Substitute sausage of choice for the hot dogs but be sure to cook them thoroughly.

Pumpkin pickles

PUMPKIN PICKLES

5 cups fresh pumpkin, peeled and cubed

2 tbsp sea salt

5 cups onions, chopped

1 tbsp pickling spice

1 cup white sugar

¼ cup white vinegar

3 bay leaves

2½ cups cold water

1 cup fresh or canned diced tomatoes

2 tbsp yellow mustard

2 tbsp cornstarch or all-purpose flour

1 tsp turmeric

6 x 250 ml Mason jars

Place the pumpkin pieces in a large bowl and sprinkle with the salt. Cover and let sit 8 hours or overnight. Drain and place the pumpkin in a stockpot or large saucepan.

Add the chopped onion to the stockpot with the pumpkin. Add the sugar, 2 cups cold water, vinegar, and bay leaves. Place the pickling spice in a piece of cheesecloth, tie it to the side of the stockpot, and drop it into the liquid.

Simmer on a medium heat for 1 hour, stirring occasionally. Stir in the tomatoes and mustard and let cook for another 5 minutes.

Combine the remaining ½ cup cold water and the cornstarch or flour in a Mason jar, shake, and then stir it into the pumpkin mixture. Add the turmeric and continue to stir until the liquid starts to thicken.

Pour into hot sterilized jars. Follow the instructions for sterilizing and canning on page 3.

RHUBARB AND STRAWBERRY JAM

4 cups rhubarb, cubed

2 cups strawberries, sliced

2 cups white sugar

1 tsp freshly squeezed lemon juice and zest

4 x 250 ml Mason jars

Combine all the ingredients in a large saucepan. Bring to a boil on a medium heat and cook for 10 to 15 minutes. Reduce the heat to low.

Continue cooking on low for 1 hour, stirring occasionally. Ensure that the mixture does not burn.

While waiting for the jam to cook, sterilize the jars and lids (see page 3).

Check the jam's readiness by spooning a teaspoonful onto a cold plate. If the jam stays thick and does not run off, scoop it into the jars.

Follow the canning procedure on page 3.

Bonita's notes

Use fresh or frozen rhubarb, fresh or frozen strawberries, and sugar of choice.

Winter fresh beef soup

Soup, Stews, and Chowders

When you're craving comfort food, don't overlook soups and stews. At least four days out of the week, Mom would make a soup or stew for supper.

She'd use a big stockpot on the wood stove, filling it to the brim with homemade soup or stew. Making soup came naturally to her—tossing in chunks of meat or salt beef to start an amazing broth. And she always served the soup with white bread, hot out of the oven, sliced and ready on the table.

If you're cooking for a big family or a crowd, this is the way to go.

BUTTERNUT SQUASH SOUP

1 butternut squash (3 to 4 lb)

1 medium potato, peeled and chopped

1 medium carrot, chopped

1 medium onion, chopped

1 medium parsnip, peeled and chopped

1 stalk celery (including leaves, for garnish), sliced

¼ tsp ground nutmeg

¼ tsp gound ginger

1 tsp sea salt

½ tsp black or white pepper

½ tsp onion powder

1 clove garlic, pressed

1 tbsp melted butter

Cut the butternut squash in half and scoop out the seeds. Sprinkle the cut side with the nutmeg and ginger. Place the squash, cut side up, on a baking sheet covered with parchment paper.

Roast the squash for 30 minutes at 350°F, cut side up; turn over and roast another 30 minutes. When fully cooked and soft, remove from the oven. Scoop the pulp out carefully into a large bowl.

Place the prepared vegetables in a saucepan. Half fill the saucepan with water, add ½ teaspoon of the salt, and bring to a boil. Simmer until the vegetables are fork-tender.

Drain the vegetables, reserving the cooking liquid, and add them to the bowl with the squash. Add about 2 cups reserved vegetable broth. Purée using a hand-held blender until the soup is smooth and silky. Add more cooking liquid, if desired. Add the melted butter, the rest of the salt, the ginger, pepper, onion powder, and garlic. Blend.

Reheat in a saucepan, if desired. To serve, top with a spoonful of sour cream (use a knife to make a design on the soup's surface) and croutons.

Bonita's notes

Adding ground nutmeg and ginger while roasting the butternut squash helps build flavour. Add more to the finished soup to taste.

Western Sandwich

- 2 eggs
- ½ cup milk or cream
- 1 slice of ham, cut in small pieces
- ¼ cup chopped bell peppers
- ¼ cup chopped green onion
- ¼ cup chopped tomato
- ½ tsp sea salt
- ½ tsp black pepper
- ½ tsp onion powder
- ½ tbsp butter
- 2 slices of cheese
- 4 slices of bread
- 1 tbsp mustard of choice
- 1 tbsp mayonnaise

This recipe makes two sandwiches.

Combine the eggs and milk or cream in a medium bowl and whisk together. Add the ham, chopped vegetables, and seasonings and combine.

Preheat a small frying pan on a medium heat and melt the butter. Add half the egg mixture and let it cook for a few minutes. Flip the eggs and continue to cook until the bottom is golden brown. Place the cheese on the top; cover with a lid to melt the cheese.

Repeat with the remaining egg.

Toast the bread. For each sandwich, spread mayonnaise on one slice and mustard on the other slice. Place an egg omelet between the two slices of bread. Cut each sandwich into four pieces.

CABBAGE SOUP (LOBSCOUSE)

- 2 pieces of salt beef, salt pork riblets, or a ham bone
- 2 cups salt beef broth (Jiggs' dinner broth, page 74)
- 6 cups water or vegetable broth
- 1 medium onion, chopped
- ½ medium cabbage, chopped (about 3 cups)
- 1 medium turnip or rutabaga, peeled and chopped
- 3 medium potatoes, peeled and chopped
- 3 medium carrots, peeled and chopped
- 1 medium parsnip, peeled and chopped
- 2 stalks celery, chopped
- ¼ cup white rice
- 1 tsp black pepper
- sea salt to taste

Soak the salt beef or riblets in cold water for 3 to 4 hours (a ham bone, if using, does not need pre-soaking). Drain, then place the meat in a stockpot. Add 2 cups salt beef broth and 6 cups cold water or vegetable broth. If you do not have salt beef broth, use more water or vegetable broth. Bring to a boil; cook for 1 hour.

Add the cabbage and cook 15 minutes. Add the remaining vegetables, rice, pepper, and salt, if desired. Cook for 30 to 45 minutes on a medium heat until the vegetables are cooked.

Serve as an appetizer or a main meal.

Bonita's notes

After all the ingredients have been added to the stockpot, stir the soup occasionally to encourage the equal cooking of all vegetables. If you don't use salt beef or salt pork riblets, or a ham bone, add 1 tablespoon sea salt to the water before adding the other ingredients.

Jiggs' dinner was traditionally cooked on Sunday. The broth, also called pot liquor, was often reserved for making soups and stews. See the recipe for Jiggs' dinner on page 74.

CARROT SOUP

- 5 large carrots, peeled and chopped
- 3 large white potato, peeled and chopped
- 1 stalk celery, chopped
- 1 large onion, diced
- 6 cups vegetable or chicken broth
- ½ tsp fresh or dried thyme
- ½ tsp white pepper
- ½ tsp sea salt
- ¼ tsp turmeric
- 1 clove garlic, grated or pressed
- 1-inch piece of ginger

Place the prepared carrots, potatoes, and celery in a bowl of cold water until ready to use.

In a frying pan, place the butter, pepper, thyme, and onion (reserve ¼ cup onion to boil with the vegetables). Fry the onion until lightly cooked. Add the garlic and fry just a few seconds more.

Place the broth, salt, ¼ cup onion, and ginger in a large saucepan. Drain the chopped vegetables and add them to the saucepan. Cook on a medium heat until fork-tender. Remove the ginger. Take the saucepan off the heat.

Add the turmeric and the fried onion mixture to the vegetables. Using a hand-held blender (or a food processor or blender), purée all ingredients until creamy.

Taste and add more thyme, salt, or pepper to taste. Pour the hot soup into serving bowls and top with a swirl of cream and croutons (page 53).

Bonita's notes

Reserving ¼ cup chopped onion to boil with the other vegetables adds extra flavour to the soup. I wait until the last few seconds of frying to add the garlic so that it doesn't burn.

Cream of turkey soup

CREAM OF TURKEY SOUP

2 cups (or more) cooked turkey, chopped

3 medium potatoes, peeled and chopped

2 medium carrots, peeled and chopped

1 small parsnip, peeled and chopped

½ small turnip or rutabaga, peeled and chopped

2 or 3 stalks celery, chopped

2 medium onions, chopped

½ cup frozen green peas

1 green onion, chopped

1 tbsp olive oil

2 tbsp butter

3 tbsp all-purpose flour

1 cup evaporated milk

4 cups vegetable broth

½ tsp black pepper

1 tsp sea salt

½ tsp dried savoury

Place the prepared potatoes, carrots, parsnip, turnip, and celery in cold water to soak until ready to use.

Sauté the chopped onions in 1 tablespoon butter and oil until tender and transparent but not golden brown. Add the flour. Cook for 1 minute, stirring constantly. Add the milk and 1 cup of the vegetable broth and stir until thickened. Simmer until ready to use.

In a large stockpot with a lid over a medium heat, place the remaining 3 cups vegetable broth and bring to a boil. Drain the prepared vegetables and add to the broth. Add the salt, pepper, and savoury. Boil 5 minutes. Add the turkey. Cook for 5 to 10 minutes more. Add the sautéed onion mixture and boil for 5 minutes.

Add 1 tablespoon butter, green onion, and green peas. Stir in and taste for seasoning. Simmer on a low heat until ready to serve.

Serve with fresh bread, rolls, or potato biscuits.

Photos on previous pages

PEA SOUP *with Doughboys*

- 1 cup chopped salt beef, salt pork riblets, or ham, or 1 ham bone (see note)
- 2 cups yellow split peas
- 1 medium onion, chopped
- 1 medium potato, peeled and chopped
- 1 cup diced celery
- ½ small turnip or rutabaga, peeled and diced
- 3 carrots, peeled and diced
- 6 cups vegetable broth or water
- ½ tsp black pepper
- 1 tbsp butter
- sea salt and pepper to taste

- 1 recipe Doughboys (page 36)

Soak the salt beef or riblets in cold water overnight. In a separate bowl, soak the split peas in cold water overnight.

Drain the salt beef. Place it in a saucepan, cover with fresh water, and simmer for about 30 minutes. Drain and cut in small pieces.

Drain the peas and place in a stockpot. Add the salt beef pieces and broth and bring to a boil. Simmer on a medium heat for 1 hour. Stir occasionally.

Then add the vegetables, pepper, and butter. Continue boiling on a medium to low heat, stirring occasionally, for another hour. Add more broth or water to reach the desired consistency.

When the peas are sufficiently soft, scoop tablespoonfuls of doughboy dough into the soup and cook for about 5 minutes, covered.

Serve topped with the pepper and fresh herbs.

Photo on next page

Bonita's notes

Peas cooked in a cotton bag with boiled Jiggs' dinner (pease pudding, page 74) can also be used to make pea soup. Just add vegetables and broth to the cooked peas, boil for about ½ hour, add the doughboy dough, and cook for another 5 minutes. The amount of salt meat used will depend on personal taste. One piece of salt beef is generally about hand-sized, and usually cooked whole and then chopped into pieces.

Doughboys

- 1½ cups all-purpose flour
- ¼ cup butter
- 3 tsp baking powder
- 1 cup cold water or milk
- 1 tsp sea salt

Cut the butter in small pieces and add to the flour, baking powder, and salt. Add the water or milk to make a soft dough. Cook as directed on page 35.

Turkey neck soup

TURKEY NECK SOUP

- turkey necks, as many as desired
- 1 piece of salt beef of choice
- 4 medium carrots, peeled and chopped
- 1 medium turnip or rutabaga, peeled and chopped
- 1 small parsnip, peeled and chopped
- 3 medium potatoes, peeled and chopped
- 3 stalks celery, chopped
- 1 medium onion, chopped
- 1 can (284 ml) tomato soup, (optional)
- ¼ cup white rice
- 1 tsp black pepper
- fresh or ground thyme to taste

Soak the salt beef overnight in a bowl of cold water. Drain and cut into small pieces.

Half fill a large stockpot with water, stock, or broth. Add the turkey necks and salt beef pieces. Bring to a boil and cook on a medium heat for 20 to 30 minutes, covered. Stir occasionally, removing any foam from the surface of the liquid.

Add the chopped vegetables to the stockpot and cook another 20 minutes.

Add the rice and the tomato soup, if using. Cook another 10 minutes or until the rice is tender.

Photo on previous page

Bonita's notes

You may substitute ham, a ham bone, or 1 tablespoon sea salt for the salt beef.
If you're including the tomato soup, rinse the can with water or broth (about half a can full) and avoid leaving any soup behind.

WINTER FRESH BEEF SOUP

6 cups broth of choice

2 lb beef cut of choice, chopped

1 medium onion, chopped

2 medium carrots, peeled and chopped

1 small parsnip, peeled and chopped

2 medium potatoes, peeled and chopped

1 small turnip, peeled and chopped

3 stalks celery, chopped

1 tsp dried thyme

1 clove garlic, chopped

1 tsp black pepper

2 tsp sea salt

2 bay leaves

¼ cup pasta or rice of choice (optional)

1 can tomato soup (284 ml) or tomato paste (156 ml)

1 tsp onion powder

Place the chopped vegetables in a bowl of cold water until needed.

Place the broth, thyme, pepper, salt, and bay leaves in a large stockpot. Bring to a boil on a medium heat. Add the chopped beef and cook for 30 minutes with the lid on, stirring occasionally.

Drain the vegetables and add to the meat and broth. Cook for another 20 to 30 minutes, stirring occasionally. Add the garlic and tomato soup or paste. Rinse the can with a little water and add that to the soup as well.

When the soup returns to a boil, add the noodles or rice. Cover and let cook for another 15 to 20 minutes. Taste and add more salt, pepper, thyme, or other seasonings, if desired. Lower the heat and let it simmer until you are ready to serve it.

Photo on page 22

BEEF STEW AND DOUGHBOYS

- 1 lb stewing beef or roast, cut into bite-sized pieces
- 1 tbsp oil
- 2 tbsp butter
- 2 to 3 tbsp flour
- 3 medium potatoes, peeled and chopped
- 1 medium onion, chopped
- 2 stalks celery, chopped
- 3 large carrots, peeled and chopped
- 1 small parsnip, peeled and chopped
- ½ small turnip or rutabaga, peeled and chopped
- 1 cup frozen green peas
- 2 cups canned diced tomatoes

>>

Preheat a large frying pan on a medium heat. Place 1 tablespoon oil and 1 tablespoon butter (more if needed) in the pan. When the butter has melted, add the beef, season with pepper, thyme, and Worcestershire sauce, and cook until brown on both sides. Add the salt and garlic and cook a few seconds more. Do not let the garlic burn.

Remove the beef from the pan and place it on a plate.

Place the chopped onion in the pan and fry until it begins to brown. Add 1 teaspoon butter and add 2 to 3 tablespoons flour, stirring. After 1 to 2 minutes, add 1 cup beef or vegetable broth. Let thicken, stirring, then set aside.

Place the vegetables, beef, and the remaining broth in a medium stockpot. Place on a medium to low heat and cook for 40 minutes. Add the tomatoes and peas and cook for another 20 minutes, stirring occasionally. Add the flour and broth mixture and continue to cook. Taste and add seasonings, if desired.

Scoop small amounts of the doughboy dough onto the surface of the stew, cover, and cook 5 more minutes.

Bonita's notes

Peel and cut all vegetables in chunks, place in a bowl of cold water, and let soak before using. Use more flour at the thickening step for a thicker stew.

<<

5 cups (or more) beef or vegetable broth

1 tsp Worcestershire sauce

½ tsp dried thyme

1 tbsp chopped garlic

½ tsp sea salt

½ tsp black pepper

1 or 2 pieces of salt beef or pork ribs (optional)

1 recipe Doughboys (page 36)

BOLOGNA STEW

2 cups cubed bologna

1 medium onion, diced

2 medium potatoes, peeled and diced

2 medium carrots, peeled and diced

1 medium turnip or rutabaga, peeled and diced

2 stalks celery, chopped

4 tbsp ketchup

2 tbsp Worcestershire sauce

½ tsp black pepper

1 tbsp butter

2 tbsp olive oil, divided

water or vegetable broth to cover

Preheat a large frying pan on a medium heat. Add the butter, 1 tablespoon olive oil, and onion. Fry until the onion starts to brown. Add the bologna and continue frying until it is golden brown. Reduce the heat to low and add the ketchup, Worcestershire sauce, and pepper. Cook for 3 to 4 minutes; remove from the heat.

Preheat a large saucepan and add 1 tablespoon olive oil. Fry the vegetables until they begin to turn golden brown. Add the bologna and onion mixture and stir to combine. Add enough hot water or broth to cover the top of the vegetables.

Continue cooking on a medium heat for about 30 minutes or until the vegetables are fork-tender. Taste; add additional ketchup, Worcestershire sauce, pepper, or salt, if desired.

Bonita's notes

This stew can also be prepared in a slow cooker on a low heat. Fry the bologna and onions, then add to the slow cooker, along with the sauces and spices. Set to a low heat and let it cook until you are ready to serve it. Serve with bread or bread rolls to soak up the sauce.

COD STEW

- 4 boneless cod fillets, chopped
- 2 medium carrots, peeled and chopped
- ½ medium turnip or rutabaga, peeled and chopped
- 3 medium potatoes, peeled and chopped
- 2 stalks celery, chopped
- 1 small parsnip, peeled and chopped
- 1 medium onion, chopped
- 1 cup cubed fat pork
- salt beef, salt pork, or sea salt to taste
- 1 tsp black pepper
- 1 tbsp butter
- 6 cups vegetable broth
- 1 tsp onion powder
- 2 tbsp all-purpose flour, plus ½ cup water for thickening
- 1 green onion, chopped

Place the prepared carrots, turnip, potatoes, celery, and parsnip in a bowl of cold water.

Melt the butter in a frying pan on a medium heat. Add the fat pork, chopped onions, onion powder, pepper, and salt beef, salt pork, or sea salt and fry until the onions are done and the pork has rendered down. (Alternatively, fry the fat pork and onions separately, removing some of the oil from the pan.) Reserve some fried fat pork (scruncheons) to garnish the finished stew.

Drain the vegetables and place them in a large stockpot with the broth. Bring to a boil on a medium heat.

Add the cod, onions, and fat pork to the stockpot and simmer for 10 minutes. Taste the broth and adjust the seasonings, if desired.

Combine the flour and water and, when the vegetables are tender, stir into the simmering stew. Cook 5 minutes.

Serve topped with green onion, pepper, and scruncheons and accompanied by homemade bread or rolls.

Bonita's notes

If you choose to use salt beef or pork, soak it overnight in cold water and drain prior to making the stew. After draining, boil the salt beef for about 1 hour in 6 to 8 cups fresh water. You may use this water in the chowder—but test for saltiness.

MUSHROOM AND GROUND BEEF STEW

1 lb lean ground beef

1 can (284 ml) whole mushrooms, or 1 cup or more sliced fresh mushrooms

1 can (284 ml) cream of mushroom soup

1 medium onion, chopped

2 medium potatoes, peeled and chopped

2 medium carrots, peeled and chopped

2 stalks celery, chopped

½ cup mixed frozen vegetables of choice

½ tsp black pepper

½ tsp sea salt

½ tsp onion powder

1 tbsp butter or oil

2 green onions, chopped

Place the prepared carrots and potatoes in a slow cooker or stockpot.

In a frying pan, fry the beef and onions in the butter or oil until the beef is cooked. Season with the salt, pepper, and onion powder. Add to the slow cooker or stockpot.

Drain the canned mushrooms, if using. If using fresh mushrooms, fry for 5 minutes, then add to the slow cooker or stockpot. Next, add the cream of mushroom soup. Rinse the can with half a can of water and pour the water into the slow cooker or stockpot as well.

Set the slow cooker to a low setting for at least 8 hours. Thirty minutes before serving, add the salt, pepper, onion powder, frozen vegetables, green onion, and celery.

If cooking on a stovetop, simmer on a medium heat for 30 minutes, then add the salt, pepper, onion powder, frozen vegetables, green onion, and celery. Cover and cook for 30 more minutes.

Serve with fresh rolls or bread and steamed rice.

Bonita's notes

Frying the ground beef and onion before adding it to the stockpot or slow cooker helps build flavours. If using fresh mushrooms, fry before adding to the stew.

Bonita's notes

As gravy browning is tasteless, it's optional. Use any browning of choice.

MEATBALL STEW

- 2 lb lean ground beef
- 1 large onion, chopped, or 280 g pearl onions
- 2 large carrots, peeled and chopped
- 1 small parsnip, peeled and chopped
- 1 small turnip or rutabaga, peeled and chopped
- 2 stalks celery, sliced
- 1 tsp black pepper
- 1 tsp sea salt
- 2 tsp dried thyme
- 1 tbsp Worcestershire sauce
- 2 tbsp all-purpose flour
- 5 cups beef broth
- 3 drops gravy browning
- 1 tsp onion powder
- 1 or 2 cloves garlic, pressed or grated
- 2 tbsp butter
- 2 tbsp olive oil

Place the prepared vegetables in a bowl of cold water until ready to use.

Place the beef in a bowl and add ½ teaspoon pepper, ½ teaspoon salt, ½ teaspoon onion powder, 1 clove garlic, and ½ teaspoon thyme. Fold the seasonings into the beef by hand. Do not overmix.

For each meatball, roll about 2 tablespoons seasoned beef into a ball. Continue until all the beef has been rolled.

Heat 1 tablespoon each of olive oil and butter in a large cast-iron frying pan. Fry the meatballs in batches until golden brown on all sides. *Do not overcrowd the pan.*

In a stockpot, bring the broth or stock to a boil on a medium heat. Drain the vegetables, add to the stockpot, and cook 10 minutes.

Add the meatballs, remaining seasonings, Worcestershire sauce, and gravy browning and continue cooking.

In the same frying pan used for the meatballs, fry the onions in 1 tablespoon butter and 1 tablespoon olive oil for 5 minutes. Mix in the flour. Add 1 cup broth from the stockpot and cook until the mixture starts to thicken. Stir the onion mixture into the simmering stew.

Cook the stew for 30 minutes on a medium to low heat, stirring occasionally. Taste and adjust seasonings, if desired.

SEAFOOD CHOWDER

3 lb boneless mixed seafood (fresh or salted cod fillets, shrimp, scallops, lobster, and salmon)

½ cup cubed salt pork

2 tbsp butter

pinch of black pepper

½ tsp sea salt

2 cups evaporated milk, heated

3 medium onions, chopped

4 medium potatoes, peeled and chopped

2 medium carrots, peeled and chopped

⅓ cup all-purpose flour

1 tbsp olive oil

1 stalk celery, cut in half

pinch of fresh dill

In a large frying pan, fry the salt pork cubes until crisp and golden brown; remove them and set aside.

In the same pan, sauté the onions until tender and transparent but not golden brown.

Place 3 cups hot water, the chopped potatoes, celery, and pepper in a large stockpot with a lid. Bring to a boil on a medium heat and cook for 5 minutes. Add the sautéed onions, boil an additional 5 minutes, then remove the celery.

Add the seafood and cook until tender, about 5 minutes.

In a small bowl or a Mason jar, combine ⅓ cup cold water and the flour until smooth. Stir into the chowder.

When the chowder starts to thicken, add 2 tablespoons butter and the heated milk and stir gently, being careful not to break up the seafood.

Top with the fried salt pork and a pinch of dill.

Bonita's notes

If you'd like to include salt cod, soak it overnight in cold water in the refrigerator. The next day, drain and cube the cod.

TOMATO SEAFOOD CHOWDER *with Croutons*

2 lb boneless mixed seafood (cod, salmon, shrimp, scallops, clams, and crab)

¼ cup cubed salt pork

1½ cups canned crushed tomatoes

1 cup canned tomato paste

3 cups vegetable broth

1 tbsp butter

1 tbsp brown sugar

1 large carrot, peeled and chopped

1 large onion, chopped

1 large white potato, peeled and chopped

1 medium parsnip, peeled and chopped

>>

In a large stockpot on a medium to high heat, stir together the butter and salt pork cubes. Fry for a few minutes to brown the cubes, then remove the scruncheons and oil from the pan.

Add the chopped vegetables, thyme, dill, pepper, salt, and sugar to the pan, and cook, stirring constantly, until the onions are tender and just starting to brown. Add the garlic.

Stir in the broth and simmer for 10 to 15 minutes until the vegetables are tender. Add the tomatoes and tomato paste and bring to a boil. Mix in the seafood and cook on a low to medium heat, stirring gently until the seafood pieces have cooked through, about 3 to 5 minutes.

Thin the chowder with more broth, if needed.

Serve piping hot, garnished with chopped fresh dill, celery leaves, thyme, scruncheons, and croutons.

Bonita's notes

Frying the fat pork pieces and then frying the vegetables in the fat will build flavour and render the oil from the far pork.

<<

2 stalks celery, chopped

2 cloves garlic, chopped

½ tsp sea salt

¼ tsp fresh or ground dill

1 tsp fresh or ground thyme

½ tsp black pepper

croutons (recipe below)

Croutons

2 slices stale bread, cubed

drizzle of olive oil

¼ tsp sea salt

¼ tsp onion powder

dash of black pepper

dash of garlic powder

Preheat the oven to 350°F. Toss the bread cubes with the seasonings and oil, then spread on a parchment-paper-lined baking sheet. Bake for 15 minutes until golden brown.

Spaghetti casserole

Casseroles

Casseroles are one of my favourite meals to plan because everything is in one dish. Just pop it in the oven, bake, and it's ready to serve.

I like to pair casseroles with a fresh tossed salad and, like Mom, I always serve it with fresh bread or rolls and a cup of hot tea.

CHEESY GOULASH CASSEROLE

- 1 lb lean ground beef
- 1 medium onion, diced
- 2 garlic cloves, pressed
- 2 cups tomato sauce of choice
- 2 tbsp olive oil
- 1 tsp sea salt
- ½ tsp black pepper
- ½ tsp dried oregano
- ½ tsp chili powder
- 1 tsp onion powder
- 2 or 3 cups elbow noodles
- 1 cup shredded cheese of choice
- 2 tbsp grated Parmesan cheese

Half fill a large saucepan with hot water. Bring to a boil and add ½ teaspoon of the salt and 1 tablespoon of the olive oil. Then add the noodles and cook only about two-thirds of the time suggested on the package. They will continue to cook in the oven.

In a frying pan with 1 tablespoon olive oil, place the beef, the remaining ½ teaspoon salt, the pepper, diced onion, onion powder, oregano, and chili powder. Fry for 10 minutes or until the beef is until no longer pink. Add the tomato sauce.

Drain the noodles, keeping 1 cup of the water for the sauce. Add the reserved water and the noodles to the frying pan; continue cooking for 5 minutes.

Pour the mixture into a 9- by 13-inch casserole dish. Top with the cheeses, cover with foil or a lid, and bake at 400°F for 20 minutes, and then another 5 to 10 minutes uncovered to brown the top.

Serve with mixed vegetables and a tossed salad.

Bonita's notes

If you use regular ground beef, drain the excess oil after frying and before adding any ingredients.

CORNED BEEF CASSEROLE

3 medium carrots, peeled and sliced

5 medium potatoes, peeled and sliced

2 medium onions, chopped

¼ medium head of cabbage, shredded

1 can (284 ml) tomato soup

1 can (340 g) corned beef, cut into chunks

½ tsp sea salt

½ tsp black pepper

½ tsp onion powder

Preheat the oven to 350°F. Place the prepared vegetables in a bowl of cold water until needed.

Pour the tomato soup into a bowl. Rinse the can with about half a can of broth or water and add it to the bowl. Mix.

Drain the vegetables. In a 9- by 13-inch casserole dish, layer the carrots, onion, cabbage, corned beef, and potatoes. Season with half the salt, pepper, and onion powder.

Pour the tomato soup over the vegetables and corned beef. Season with the remaining salt, pepper, and onion powder. Cover with a lid or foil. Bake for 2 hours.

Serve with fresh bread rolls or bread sticks and sour cream.

Bonita's notes

This can also be cooked in a slow cooker on a low setting or in a roasting pan on the barbecue. Set the barbecue to a low to medium heat and let it cook 1 hour, or more if needed.

DOUBLE BAKED POTATO CASSEROLE

6 large potatoes, peeled and cut into chunks

1 tsp sea salt

¼ cup butter

½ tsp white pepper

1 cup sour cream

2 tbsp cream cheese

4 to 6 strips fried bacon, chopped

1 green onion, chopped

1 cup shredded cheddar cheese

Place the potatoes in a large saucepan and cover with water. Add the salt. Bring to a boil and cook until they are tender.

Drain the potatoes and place in a large bowl. Add the butter, pepper, sour cream, and cream cheese, and mash.

Add half the bacon pieces, green onion, and cheddar cheese to the potatoes. Fold in.

Scoop the potatoes into a casserole dish (8 inches in diameter or larger) spread evenly and top with the remaining cheddar cheese, green onion, and bacon.

Bake at 350°F for 35 to 40 minutes or until golden brown.

Bonita's notes

Boiling the potatoes speeds up the cooking process, but you can bake them if you prefer.
Try with other cheeses. This dish can also be baked in the barbecue in a roaster with a lid.
Chop just the green part of the green onion for this recipe. Place the onion buds in ¼ cup cold water and leave on the countertop or a windowsill to continue growing. Change the water daily.

LASAGNA ROLL-UPS

12 lasagna noodles

1 lb lean ground beef, pork, or chicken

1 medium onion, chopped

2 cups cooked white rice

3 cups pasta sauce of choice

1 tsp black pepper

1 tsp sea salt

1 tsp onion powder

1 medium carrot, peeled and grated

1 cup shredded cheese of choice

½ cup Parmesan cheese

1 tbsp olive oil

1 garlic clove, pressed

½ cup chopped tomatoes

2 green onions, chopped

Cook the noodles in a stockpot of hot water with ½ teaspoon of the salt. Follow the cooking instructions on the box, but cook 1 minute less than suggested.

Fry the beef in the oil on a medium heat. Add the onion, ½ teaspoon of the salt, the pepper, garlic, and onion powder. Continue frying until the beef is thoroughly cooked.

In a large bowl, combine the beef and onion mixture, rice, carrot, and 1 cup of the pasta sauce. Toss together.

Working with one lasagna noodle at a time, scoop ½ cup beef-onion mixture onto one end and slowly roll outward. Place in an 11- by 8-inch (or larger) casserole dish. Continue filling and rolling all the noodles, placing them side by side in the dish. Top with the remaining pasta sauce, shredded cheese, Parmesan cheese, tomatoes, and green onion.

Bake at 375°F for 40 minutes to 1 hour. Cover the pan with foil for the first 30 minutes, then uncover and continue to bake until golden brown.

Serve with more pasta sauce, fresh rolls or garlic bread, and a tossed salad.

Photos on next pages

Bonita's notes

Cooking the ground beef and rice first speeds up baking time. Undercooking the lasagna noodles will prevent them from being overcooked in the oven.

Lasagna roll-ups

JOIN US
BY THE SEA
Bonita's
Kitchen

SEVEN-LAYER DINNER

3 medium potatoes, peeled and thinly sliced

3 medium onions, thinly sliced

3 medium carrots, peeled and thinly sliced

¼ cup uncooked rice of choice

1 cup canned or frozen peas

1½ lb sausage of choice

1 can (284 ml) tomato soup

1 tsp sea salt

1 tsp black pepper

Place the prepared vegetables in separate bowls of cold water. Drain when ready to assemble the casserole.

Grease a deep casserole dish and start layering, seasoning each layer with salt and pepper: first the potatoes, then the onions, carrots, rice, and green peas.

In a frying pan, partly cook the sausages. Cut into bite-sized pieces and add to the casserole dish.

Pour the tomato soup over the layers. Rinse the can with 1 cup cold water, and pour on the layers.

Top with a sprinkle of salt and pepper. Cover the dish with foil and bake at 350°F for 1 hour or until tender.

Serve with fresh bread rolls.

Bonita's notes

This recipe features the ingredients Dad would use when making this meal. Use more or different seasonings in this dish, according to your taste.

Partially cooking the sausage removes any excess oil—but you do want to include some in the casserole.

SPAGHETTI CASSEROLE

- 1 box (16 oz) spaghetti
- 1 lb lean ground beef
- 1 large onion, chopped
- 2 to 3 cups pasta sauce of choice
- 1 tsp sea salt
- 1 tsp black pepper
- 1 tsp onion powder
- 1 tsp garlic powder
- 2 large eggs
- 2 cups cottage cheese
- 2 cups shredded mozzarella cheese
- ¼ cup Parmesan cheese, plus more for topping
- ¼ cup melted butter
- 3 tbsp olive oil
- 1 tsp ground or fresh oregano
- 1 tomato, sliced
- 2 small sweet peppers (any colour), sliced

Half fill a saucepan with water. Add 1 tablespoon of the olive oil and ½ teaspoon of the salt and bring to a boil on a medium heat.

Add the spaghetti to the boiling water and cook for about 8 minutes; it should be just undercooked. Drain, reserving ½ cup of the pasta water. In a bowl, toss the spaghetti with about 1 tablespoon olive oil.

Place 1 tablespoon olive oil, the ground beef, ½ teaspoon of the salt, the pepper, onion powder, and garlic powder in a large frying pan. Fry for 3 or 4 minutes, then add the onion and cook until the beef is no longer pink. Fold in the pasta sauce and pasta water, warm through, then turn off the heat.

Whisk the eggs in a medium bowl and pour over the spaghetti. Add the Parmesan cheese and melted butter and toss again.

In a large casserole dish or 9- by 13-inch baking pan, layer all the ingredients: half of the spaghetti, 1 cup cottage cheese, half of the meat sauce, 1 cup mozzarella cheese, a pinch of oregano, and a few slices of peppers. Repeat.

Top with the tomato and pepper slices. Sprinkle with a pinch of oregano and Parmesan cheese. Cover with aluminum foil.

Bake at 350°F for 30 minutes. Remove the aluminum foil and bake another 30 minutes, longer if needed.

Serve with fresh bread.

Photo on page 54

Bonita's notes

If you use medium ground beef, drain all the oil from it before adding the onions.
Seasoning the hot water with salt and oil keeps the spaghetti from sticking together and it also salts the spaghetti.

Meat and vegetable pastry

Pastries

Making pastry for a savoury dish is just like making it for a sweet pie crust. Once you've made the pastry, roll it into a ball and place it in the refrigerator to allow the butter to harden.

After it has chilled, roll out the pastry to cover a roast or make smaller pastries for individual meals.

Here are some tasty pastry recipes you can whip up in no time. They're affordable, and you can even roll them out and freeze them for another day.

JIGGS' DINNER PASTRY

Pastry

2 cups white or whole wheat flour, plus more for dusting

½ cup cold butter

½ tsp sea salt

½ cup cold water

The pastry recipe and method for making the filled pastries below is followed by recipes for Jiggs' dinner with pease pudding, gravy, blueberry duff, roasted chicken, and stuffing—these are delicious recipes on their own, and can be combined as filling for the pastry.

Mix the flour, butter, and salt in a food processor or by hand in a bowl. When the butter has been worked into the flour, add the cold water slowly, until the mixture shapes into a ball. Remove from the bowl or mixer and cut in half.

Place a piece of parchment paper on the counter and dust with flour.

Roll out the pastry on the parchment and cut into 4-inch squares. Place one piece of each Jiggs' dinner element on each square, including any or all of potato, carrot, turnip, parsnip, cabbage, salt beef, pease pudding, chicken or roast beef, stuffing, and blueberry duff. Fold the pastry over on all sides and pinch together.

Place the filled pastries on a parchment-paper-covered baking sheet. Crack 1 egg in a bowl, whisk, and brush over the pastry (or use melted butter instead).

Bake the filled pastries at 350°F for 30 to 40 minutes or until golden brown.

Remove and serve hot with gravy.

Bonita's notes

This recipe can easily be doubled. If you are using salted butter, don't add salt.
If you make this pasty in advance, keep it rolled up and covered in plastic in the refrigerator for a day or two, or freeze for longer.
These freeze well in a freezer bag or container for lunches. Reheat in an air fryer for 5 minutes, or oven for 15 minutes.

Bonita's
Kitchen

Jiggs' Dinner with Pease Pudding

1 or 2 pieces of salt beef or salt pork riblets

6 medium potatoes, peeled and halved

1 medium head of cabbage, quartered

1 medium turnip, peeled and sliced

6 medium carrots, peeled and halved

1 small parsnip, peeled and halved

1 medium onion

450 g yellow split peas

1 tbsp butter

black pepper to taste

Soak the salt beef overnight in cold water. Drain. Place the beef in a large stockpot, cover with cold water, and add the onion. (As a faster alternative to soaking the beef, boil it in a large stockpot for 30 minutes, drain, and proceed.)

Pour the peas into a pudding bag, tie with cotton string, and soak overnight in cold water. Drain and place the bag in the stockpot with the beef and onion. Tie the pudding bag to the side of the stockpot.

Bring the water to a boil and simmer the beef and peas for about 1 hour. Check to see if the peas are the desired consistency. At this point, remove the pudding bag from the pot or leave it in the water to further cook with the vegetables.

Add the cabbage and turnip to the stockpot and boil for 15 minutes. Add the potatoes, carrot, and parsnip and boil for another 15 minutes, or until the potatoes are fork-tender.

Remove the bag from the stockpot, cut the string, and pour the peas into a bowl. Add the butter and pepper to taste.

Remove all the vegetables from the stockpot and put in separate bowls.

Reserve the pot liquid for gravy or soup broth.

Roasted Chicken with Dressing (Stuffing)

1 3- to 4-lb chicken

3 cups bread crumbs

1 medium onion, chopped

1 tbsp melted butter or olive oil

1 tbsp dried savoury

pinch of sea salt

pinch of black pepper

½ cup vegetable broth

Wash the chicken in cold water. Dry the interior and exterior with a paper towel. Place the chicken in a roaster or other oven-safe pan.

Mix the crumbs, half of the onion, and the butter or olive oil. Add the savoury, salt, and pepper. Combine by hand.

Fill the chicken cavity with the dressing. Top the chicken with salt, pepper, and the remaining onion. Pour the broth into the pan and cover. Bake at 350°F for 2 hours or until golden brown, checking it every 30 minutes to baste with its drippings.

When it is fully cooked, remove the chicken from the roaster, place it on a plate, and cover. Put the roaster on the stovetop to make the gravy.

Gravy from Chicken Drippings

chicken drippings

1 cup (or more) vegetable broth or Jiggs' dinner pot liquid

1 tsp gravy browning or Oxo cube

¼ cup all-purpose flour or cornstarch

1 cup cold water

Whisk the broth and gravy browning into the chicken drippings in the roaster and let it come to a boil.

Combine the flour or cornstarch and cold water in a Mason jar. Cover and shake well until all the lumps have dissolved. Pour into the boiling broth and stir until it starts to thicken.

Caramel Sauce

2 tbsp butter

1 cup dark brown sugar

1 tbsp vanilla

¼ cup evaporated milk or milk

Melt the butter in a saucepan. Add the sugar and vanilla and whisk to combine. Cook on a low heat, stirring constantly, until the mixture thickens. Do not allow it to simmer, as it may curdle.

Whisk in the milk and remove from the heat.

Whisk before serving. The sauce should be soft, creamy, and smooth.

Microwave-style Blueberry Duff

- ¼ cup butter, melted
- ½ cup white sugar
- pinch of sea salt
- 1 egg, beaten
- ¼ cup milk
- 1 cup all-purpose flour, plus more for tossing with the berries
- 1½ tsp baking powder
- ½ tsp vanilla
- 1 cup fresh or frozen blueberries

Pour the melted butter into a microwaveable mixing bowl and swirl to coat the bowl.

In a separate bowl, cream the butter and sugar until light and fluffy. Stir in the egg, milk, vanilla, and dry ingredients. In another bowl, toss the blueberries in flour, then fold into the mixture.

Scoop the batter into the buttered microwaveable bowl, smooth the top, and cover with a plate.

Microwave for about 6 minutes at full power. Using oven mitts, lift the plate carefully to avoid being burned by any escaping steam. Loosen the sides of the duff with a spatula. Tip it onto the plate and allow it to cool. Serve with caramel sauce (recipe page 76).

PORK TENDERLOIN WITH PASTRY

- 2 lb pork tenderloin
- 1 medium onion, chopped
- 2 cups fresh or frozen spinach (thawed)
- 2 eggs
- 2 tbsp Mother's Mustard Sauce (page 8) or mustard of choice
- 1 cup feta cheese
- 1 tsp sea salt
- 1 tsp black or white pepper
- 1 tsp onion powder
- 1 tsp dried thyme
- 1 tbsp olive oil
- 2 apples, cut in wedges
- 1 recipe pastry (page 72)

Cut the silver skin and fat off the tenderloin and then butterfly it by cutting it in half, but not all the way through.

Place the spinach in a bowl. If working with thawed spinach, remove as much water as possible by pinching and squeezing the leaves. Add the chopped onion, feta, and half of the salt, pepper, and onion powder, and toss together. Add 1 egg and the Mother's Mustard Sauce or mustard and mix well.

Spread the spinach mixture on the middle of the tenderloin.

Roll or fold the tenderloin and season with the remainder of the salt, pepper, and onion powder.

In a frying pan on a medium heat, place the butter and olive oil and fry the tenderloin until it is golden brown on all sides, or for 10 minutes. Remove the tenderloin from the pan and let it come to room temperature. Add the apple wedges to the frying pan and fry just to brown. Keep warm to serve with the tenderloin.

Make the pastry and roll out.

Place the partially cooked tenderloin in the centre of the pastry and fold the pastry around it. Make four cuts in the pastry.

In a small bowl, whisk the remaining egg, then brush it on the pastry.

Place the pastry-covered tenderloin on a parchment-paper-lined baking sheet. Bake at 400°F until the pastry is golden brown and the tenderloin registers an internal temperature of 145°F to 150°F on a meat thermometer.

Serve with gravy, fried apple wedges, and steamed or baked vegetables of choice.

Bonita's notes

Be sure to remove the tough silver skin from the tenderloin. Remove any extra fat to ensure the pastry doesn't become soggy.

Bonita's notes

Double the pastry recipe to make a dozen pastries.
Let the meat mixture come to room temperature before filling the pastries.

MEAT AND VEGETABLE PASTRIES

- 1 lb lean ground beef
- 1 medium onion, chopped
- 1 medium carrot, peeled and cubed
- 1 medium potato, peeled and cubed
- ½ small turnip, peeled and cubed
- 2 tbsp all-purpose flour
- 1 cup vegetable broth
- 1 tsp beef bouillon powder or Oxo cube
- ½ tsp black pepper
- ½ tsp sea salt
- ½ tsp onion powder
- 2 cloves garlic, chopped
- 1 tbsp olive oil
- 1 tbsp melted butter

- 1 recipe pastry (page 72)

Place the prepared vegetables in a bowl of cold water to soak until needed.

In a medium frying pan on a medium heat, fry the beef in olive oil. After 2 or 3 minutes, add the onions, bouillon, pepper, and onion powder and continue frying until the beef has browned.

Add the garlic and continue to fry for 1 minute. Add the flour, toss, then add the vegetable broth and mix well. Lower the heat until it is ready for the next step.

Bring a medium saucepan half filled with water to a boil, then add the salt. Drain the vegetables, add to the hot salted water, and boil until tender.

Drain the vegetables. Add the vegetables to the fried beef and mix. Add more broth if needed—the mixture should be moist but not runny. Let it cool.

Make the pastry and cut the dough ball into six pieces. Roll each piece into an oval about 6 inches long.

Place about ½ cup of the meat and vegetable mixture on one side of each oval. Flip the other end of the pastry over the top and pinch the edges to seal. Place all the pastries on a parchment-paper-lined baking sheet. Brush the tops with melted butter.

Bake at 375°F for about 40 minutes or until the pastry is golden.

Serve hot with gravy or cool and wrap for school or work lunches. These can be easily rewarmed or are delicious eaten cold.

Photo on page 70

ROAST AND DUFF

- 1 beef roast (any size or cut)
- 1 medium onion, chopped
- 1 stalk celery, chopped
- 1 tbsp butter or oil
- 2 cups beef or vegetable broth or stock
- ½ cup all-purpose flour or 1 tbsp cornstarch
- 1 cup water
- sea salt to taste
- black pepper to taste
- rosemary to taste

- 1 recipe Duff Pastry (see 83)

Season the beef on both sides with the salt, pepper, and rosemary, then place in a hot frying pan with the butter or oil. Fry the beef on each side to brown it, about 10 minutes. Remove the beef from the pan and place it in a roaster.

Sauté the onions and celery in the same frying pan until soft, then add to the roaster, along with the broth or stock. Sprinkle with salt and pepper and cover. Roast for 25 minutes at 425°F. Reduce the heat to 375°F for 16 minutes per pound or until tender, the last 20 minutes of cooking time remove from heat and let rest. This will be a medium cooked roast. If you prefer the beef to be falling apart, continue to roast at 375°F, covered, until fork-tender.

Remove the beef and set on a plate to rest while making the gravy.

Set the roaster on the stovetop on a medium heat and bring the broth to a boil. Shake the water and flour or cornstarch in a Mason jar until thoroughly combined. Pour into the roaster and stir until the gravy thickens. Return the beef to the roaster with the gravy. If desired, pour out some gravy to serve with the vegetables.

Drape the rolled-out duff pastry on the beef and gravy and return the roaster to the oven. Do not cover. Bake for 15 to 20 minutes or until the pastry is golden brown.

Cut the duff into tea-bun-sized pieces and serve with the beef and gravy. Enjoy with boiled vegetables, carrot, turnip, and potatoes.

Photos on pages 84 and 85

Duff Pastry

- 2 cups all-purpose or whole wheat flour, plus more for sprinkling
- ⅓ cup white sugar
- 4 tsp baking powder
- ¼ tsp sea salt
- ½ cup cold butter, cut in small pieces
- ½ cup evaporated milk
- 1 egg

Combine the dry ingredients in a bowl. Add the butter and mix by hand until the mixture is crumbly.

Combine the egg and milk in a separate bowl and add to the mixture, working it in by hand or stand mixer with a dough hook until the dough forms a ball.

Place the dough ball on a piece of waxed or parchment paper on the counter. Sprinkle with flour and roll out to the size of the beef top. Follow the instructions on page 82 to bake.

Bonita's notes

The duff pastry can be used to top any roast or stew. Just be sure that the meat or stew is almost cooked (and the gravy made) before covering it with the pastry.
Make extra gravy to serve with the roast and duff.

Roast and duff

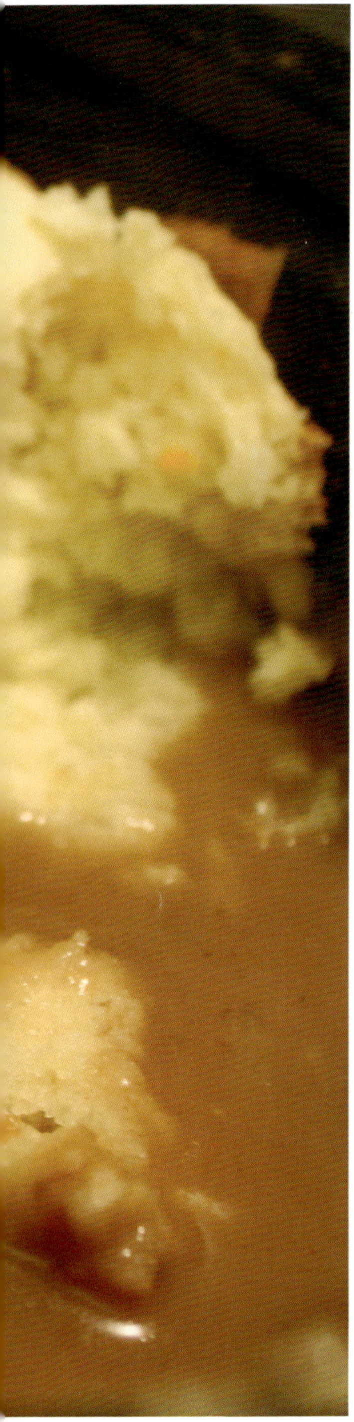

TURKEY PASTRIES

- 2 cups chopped cooked turkey or chicken
- 1 cup shredded cheese of choice
- 2 tbsp all-purpose flour or cornstarch, plus more for sprinkling
- 2 tbsp butter
- ½ tsp black pepper
- ½ tsp sea salt
- ½ cup chicken or vegetable broth
- ½ cup milk of choice or cream
- 1 medium onion, chopped
- 1 garlic clove, pressed or grated
- 1 cup mixed frozen vegetables

- 1 recipe pastry (page 72)

Place the butter in a large saucepan on a medium heat and let it melt. Add the onion and fry until it is partially cooked. Add the flour or cornstarch and stir to combine. Add the broth, salt, pepper, garlic, and milk. Continue stirring until the sauce starts to thicken.

Add the vegetables and turkey or chicken and fold together until it is well coated.

Cut the pastry dough ball into six pieces. Place a piece of parchment paper on the counter, sprinkle with flour, then roll each piece out into an oval about 6 inches long on the floured paper.

Scoop about ½ cup of the turkey filling onto one side of the pastry, fold the other end over the mixture, and pinch the sides together. Continue with the remaining dough. Place the pastries on a parchment-paper-lined baking sheet.

Grease the tops of the pastries and bake in a preheated 375°F oven for 40 minutes until golden brown.

Serve with gravy. Or let the pastries cool and wrap them for school or work lunches.

Bonita's notes

Having all ingredients measured and ready before starting makes this recipe a snap.
Making the pastry beforehand and letting it cool in the refrigerator helps to ensure flakier pastry.

CORNED BEEF PASTRIES

- 4 medium potatoes, peeled and quartered
- 1 medium onion, chopped
- 1 can (340 g) corned beef
- ½ to 1 tsp pepper
- ½ tsp dried savoury
- ½ to 1 tsp sea salt for boiling the potatoes
- 1 tbsp butter
- 1 tsp olive oil
- 1 recipe pastry (page 72)

Rinse the potatoes in cold water or soak for a few minutes to remove some of the starch, then drain.

Place the potatoes and salt in a medium saucepan half full of hot water and boil on a medium heat until fork-tender. Drain.

Chop the corned beef and place in a bowl.

Place the butter and oil in a medium frying pan on a medium heat. Add the onions, pepper, and savoury. Fry until the onions are soft and golden brown.

Combine the potatoes, corned beef, and onions in a bowl. Mash together and set aside until ready to use.

Make the pastry as outlined on page 72. Cut the dough in half. Place a piece of parchment on the counter and dust with flour. Roll out half the dough. Use a 3½- to 4-inch round cookie cutter to cut 12 pieces of pastry. From the extra pastry, cut out small half moons for garnish.

Butter or spray (with baking oil) a 12-cup muffin pan, then place a circle of pastry in each cup. Top with the corned beef mixture and, if desired, a pastry half moon. Bake in a preheated 350°F oven for 20 to 25 minutes or until golden brown.

Bonita's notes

These freeze well. Allow them to cool to room temperature before placing them in a freezer bag or container.

Upper Island Cove

Salads

When I was growing up, the tradition in our family was to peel and soak all the vegetables on Saturday night for Sunday dinner and supper. We'd make potato salads, coleslaw, dressing for the chicken, and soak the salted beef for the Jiggs' dinner. We'd also bake a dessert and one or two batches of bread. Sunday was a day for resting, visiting family, and going to church, so we did everything we could on Saturday.

COLD PLATES *with Potato Salads and Coleslaw*

- leftover turkey or chicken
- turkey or chicken stuffing
- tomato slices
- lettuce leaves
- turkey roll
- sliced ham
- cheese of choice
- pickles
- bread roll with butter

Make the coleslaw and other salads (recipes follow) and refrigerate until it is time to plate. Get creative! Anything can go on a cold plate:

For each cold plate: 2 scoops of each salad, 1 scoop of coleslaw, a few lettuce leaves, tomato slices, roast chicken or turkey and stuffing, rolled-up ham and turkey roll, cheese, and a bread roll.

Beet Potato Salad

6 medium potatoes, peeled and cut in large pieces

1 medium onion, halved

½ tsp sea salt

1 cup chopped pickled beets

½ cup mayonnaise

¼ cup juice from the bottle of pickled beets

1 tbsp white sugar

2 large eggs

sprinkle of paprika

Topping

¼ cup mayonnaise

1 tbsp beet juice

Place the potatoes, onion halves, and salt in a medium saucepan half filled with water. Boil until the potatoes are fork-tender, drain, and mash. Discard the onion or mash with the potatoes. Add the beet juice and sugar and mash until all the ingredients are combined.

Hard-boil the eggs, for about 10 minutes, in a small saucepan half filled with water. Drain and peel. Mash 1 egg with the potatoes; slice the remaining egg and set aside.

Mix the mayonnaise into the mashed potatoes until creamy.

Combine the topping ingredients in a small bowl.

Scoop the salad into a large bowl and spread the topping evenly on the salad. Arrange the egg slices on the top, sprinkle with paprika, and refrigerate.

Bonita's notes

Mash the potatoes while they are hot and allow to come to room temperature before mixing in the mayonnaise. Potato salad can be refrigerated for up to 3 days.

Mustard Potato Salad

6 medium potatoes, peeled and chopped

1 medium onion, halved

2 eggs

½ tsp sea salt

1 tbsp white sugar

1 tbsp white vinegar

½ cup yellow mustard

1 tbsp cream or evaporated milk

1 tbsp butter

½ cup mayonnaise

Topping

¼ cup mayonnaise

¼ cup yellow mustard

Place the potato, onion, and salt in a medium saucepan half filled with water. Boil until the potatoes are fork-tender; drain. Discard the onion or mash it with the potatoes.

Add the butter and cream to the potatoes and mash thoroughly. Add the mustard, vinegar, and sugar and continue mashing. Mix in the ¼ cup mayonnaise until creamy.

Hard-boil the eggs, about 10 minutes. Drain and peel. Mash 1 egg with the potatoes; slice the remaining egg and set it aside until needed.

Combine the topping ingredients. Spread on the salad and top with the egg slices. Refrigerate until ready to serve.

Coleslaw

2 cups shredded white cabbage

1 large carrot, peeled and shredded

2 tbsp white vinegar

½ cup mayonnaise

sea salt and black pepper to taste

2 tsp sugar

Combine the shredded carrot and cabbage in a medium bowl with a lid.

Whisk together the remaining ingredients to make the dressing in a separate bowl. Toss the dressing with the cabbage-carrot mixture and refrigerate until ready to serve.

Bonita's notes

If making this ahead of time, don't add the dressing until 1 to 2 hours before serving. Once assembled, serve the coleslaw within 3 days.

LOBSTER SALAD

3 cups chopped cooked lobster

4 large hard-boiled eggs, quartered

1 small onion, grated

¼ cup relish of choice

¼ cup mayonnaise

10 cherry tomatoes, cut in half

2 green onions, sliced

½ tsp sea salt

½ tsp black pepper

½ tsp onion powder

1 tbsp olive oil

1 stalk celery, chopped

½ tsp dried or 2 tsp fresh dill

Combine the mayonnaise, oil, relish, salt, pepper, and onion powder to make the dressing.

Place the chopped lobster in a glass bowl and add the eggs, onion, and tomatoes. Add the dressing and toss.

Add the green onion, celery, and dill. Toss again and refrigerate until ready to serve.

Photos on next pages

Bonita's notes

Freshly cooked lobster is preferred, but this salad is also delicious when made with crab, shrimp, or canned lobster. Make this on the day you are going to serve it.

Lobster salad

MAPLE-GLAZED SALMON *with Tossed Salad and Dollar Fries*

2 4-oz salmon fillets, skin on

1 cup maple syrup

1 or 2 cloves garlic, crushed

1 tbsp butter

1 tbsp olive oil

sea salt to taste

black pepper to taste

lemon wedges for garnish

Warm a large cast-iron frying pan on a low heat, and add the oil and butter. Season the salmon on both sides with the salt and pepper. Let rest for 5 to 10 minutes at room temperature. Meanwhile, combine the maple syrup and garlic in a small bowl.

Raise the heat of the frying pan to medium-high. Place the salmon in the pan, skin side up, and fry for 4 minutes, until the flesh is golden brown. Flip the salmon and fry for 3 to 4 minutes, until the skin is crisp.

Pour the maple syrup mixture over the salmon, cover the pan, and turn off the heat and let it rest for 2 minutes.

Place the salmon on a plate and pour the sauce over it. Serve with a tossed salad and dollar fries (recipes follow).

Photos on next pages

Tossed Salad

1 head romaine lettuce, washed and chopped

2 carrots, peeled and shredded

Toss the lettuce and carrots. Serve with dressings (recipes on page 103).

Dollar Fries

2 large white potatoes, peeled if desired

Slice the potatoes, dry well, and pan- or deep-fry until they are golden brown. Sprinkle with a pinch of salt.

Bonita's notes

Pour the herb and garlic dressing over the tossed salad first; top with a scoop of the feta dressing.

Maple-glazed salmon with herb and feta salad

Herb and Garlic Dressing

¼ cup balsamic vinegar

¼ cup olive oil

1 tsp fresh or ground ginger

3 cloves garlic, chopped

½ cup maple syrup

6 tsp soy sauce

½ tsp dried or 2 tsp fresh dill

¼ tsp black pepper

Whisk all the ingredients together. Adjust the amounts to taste. This dressing can be refrigerated for up to 1 week. Makes 1 cup.

Feta and Dill Dressing

¼ cup plain Greek yogurt

2 cloves garlic, pressed

½ cup feta cheese

1 tbsp olive oil

1 tbsp lemon juice

1 tbsp liquid honey

pinch of black pepper

½ tsp dried or 2 tsp fresh dill

Combine the yogurt, garlic, feta, and lemon juice. Add the honey, pepper, and dill. Slowly pour in the oil and whisk together until all the ingredients are well mixed.

CHUNKY HOT POTATO SALAD

4 to 6 potatoes, peeled and diced

2 large eggs

1 small onion, chopped

1 small sweet pepper, any colour, chopped

¼ cup white vinegar

2 tbsp butter or oil

1 tsp sea salt

½ to 1 tsp black pepper

1 tsp white sugar

1 tsp onion powder

Optional garnishes
sliced green onions, fresh parsley, paprika, and/or bacon bits

Soak the potatoes in cold water for 5 minutes to remove some of the starch. Drain. Place the potatoes in a saucepan half filled with water and boil them with a pinch of salt until they are fork-tender; drain.

Fry the onion and sweet pepper lightly in the butter until tender. Add the vinegar, salt, pepper, and sugar and cook for another 2 or 3 minutes.

Crack the eggs into a bowl and whisk. Add a scoop of the onion-pepper mixture to the beaten eggs, whisk, then pour the eggs into the frying pan. Stir in the rest of the onion-pepper mixture. Add the hot diced potatoes. Mix lightly and lower the heat.

Scoop the hot potato salad into a serving bowl. Garnish as desired and serve with fresh bread and pickles.

Bonita's notes

Add chopped hard-boiled eggs, either regular or pickled, to the salad for additional taste and texture.

Bacon-wrapped stuffed cod

Seafood

There's nothing like a good feed of fish. Seafood is not only good for you but it makes for incredibly tasty meals, whether it's baked, roasted, grilled, covered in sauce, or deep-fried.

BACON-WRAPPED STUFFED COD

- 6 cod fillets, skinned and deboned
- 6 strips of bacon
- 4 cups bread crumbs
- 1 tbsp dried savoury
- pinch of sea salt
- pinch of black pepper
- 1 small onion, grated
- 1 tbsp butter or oil

Rinse the cod fillets and pat dry with a paper towel.

Combine the bread crumbs, savoury, salt, pepper, butter, and onion and set aside.

Season the cod with salt and pepper on both sides. Place about ¼ cup of the stuffing on each fillet, pat it down, and roll up the fillet. Wrap a piece of bacon around each fillet and place them in a deep pan or on a baking sheet lined with parchment paper to catch the oil that is released from the bacon.

Place in a preheated 350°F oven for 30 to 45 minutes or until the bacon is golden brown.

Serve with drawn butter (recipe follows), rice, and vegetables of choice.

Drawn Butter

- 1 tbsp butter or oil
- 2 tbsp all-purpose flour or cornstarch
- 1 cup vegetable broth or stock
- 1 cup chopped onion
- sea salt and black pepper to taste

Fry the butter and onions in a cast-iron frying pan on a medium heat. Add the salt and pepper. When the onions have started to soften, add the flour and stir it in until the onions are cooked.

Add the broth and stir until the mixture starts to thicken. Reduce the heat and simmer for several minutes, until the desired consistency is reached.

BEER-BATTERED COD

- 2 cod fillets, skinned, deboned, and cut in 8 small pieces
- 1 cup all-purpose flour
- 1 tbsp garlic powder
- ½ tbsp paprika
- 1 tsp sea salt
- 1 tsp onion powder
- 1 tbsp black pepper
- ½ tsp celery salt
- ½ tsp dried thyme
- 1 tbsp ketchup
- 1 large egg
- 1 can (355 ml) beer of choice

Rinse the cod with cold water, pat dry with a paper towel, and season with salt and pepper.

Combine the flour, spices, ketchup, and egg in a large bowl. Stir in the beer. Place all the cod pieces in the beer batter and coat evenly.

Preheat the deep fryer to 350°F. Slowly place 2 pieces of cod in the hot oil. *Don't overcrowd the fryer.*

Fry the cod for 5 minutes on each side until golden brown, then place on a paper-towel-lined plate. Continue until all the cod has been fried.

Bonita's notes

Serve hot to keep the crust crispy, with the side dish of choice. Keep uncovered in a 250°F oven until ready to serve.

BUBBLY FISH BAKE

- 1 lb cod or other white fish, skinned and deboned
- 1 can (284 ml) cream of mushroom soup
- 2 tbsp chopped onion
- 1 tbsp lemon juice
- 1 cup grated cheddar cheese, or more to taste
- 3 tbsp milk of choice
- 1 cup bread crumbs or crushed soda crackers
- sea salt, black pepper, and onion powder to taste

Season the cod on both sides with the salt, pepper, and onion powder and place in a greased 8-inch casserole dish.

Season the bread crumbs with sea salt, pepper, and onion powder.

Combine the soup, onion, lemon juice, and milk; pour over the cod. Top with the cheese and bread crumbs.

Bake in a preheated 450°F oven for 20 minutes or until bubbly and golden brown on top.

Recipe by my friend Trixie Williams of Pools Cove, NL.

COD AU GRATIN

- 2 cod fillets (about 1 lb), skin and bones removed
- 1 medium onion, chopped
- 3 tbsp butter
- 1 tbsp olive oil
- 6 tbsp all-purpose flour
- 2 cups milk
- 1 cup shredded cheese of choice
- 1 tbsp sliced green onion
- pinch of sea salt and black pepper
- pinch of dried dill, thyme, or herb of choice

Grease a 9- by 9-inch baking dish or 6 small ramekins or serving dishes. Bring 4 cups water and a pinch of salt to a boil. Add the cod, and boil for 5 to 10 minutes to partially cook it. Drain.

Melt the butter with the olive oil in a medium saucepan. Add the onion and fry until soft. Remove the saucepan from the heat and whisk in the flour and milk. Return to the heat and continue cooking until the sauce has thickened, whisking frequently. Season with salt and pepper. Add more milk or liquid from the cooked cod if needed.

Flake the cod and remove all bones. Place the cod in the baking dish or divide it equally among smaller dishes. Pour the sauce over each and mix through.

Top with the cheese, salt. and pepper. Bake in a preheated 350°F oven for 20 minutes or until golden brown.

Garnish with the green onion and herbs.

Serve with steamed rice or baby potatoes.

Photos on next pages

Bonita's notes

Cheese can be added to the sauce mixture and the dish topped with bread crumbs before it is baked.

Cod au gratin

COD BITES

2 cod fillets (about 1 lb or 2 cups cooked cod), skin and bones removed

1½ cups chopped peeled potatoes

¼ medium onion

1 egg, beaten

1 tbsp butter

½ tsp sea salt

½ tsp black pepper

1 tbsp grated onion

1 tbsp all-purpose flour

1 lemon, cut in wedges

1 cup bottled cocktail sauce

Half fill a saucepan with water. Add a pinch of salt and the onion quarter and bring to a boil. Add the cod and simmer for 5 minutes on a medium heat, drain, and flake. Use 2 or more cups in this recipe.

Half fill another saucepan with water; add the potatoes and a pinch of salt and boil until fork-tender. Drain and mash with the butter and pepper. Add the grated onion and continue mashing.

Add the flaked cod to the mashed potatoes and mix with a fork until creamy. Let the mixture cool to room temperature. Add the egg and flour and continue creaming together. If the mixture is soft, refrigerate to cool further before using.

Shape the cod-potato mixture into tablespoon-sized balls. Heat the deep fryer to 350°F to 400°F. Fry 4 or 5 balls at a time until golden brown. Drain on a paper towel to remove the excess oil.

Serve with cocktail sauce and lemon wedges.

Bonita's notes

Peeling the potatoes and soaking them in cold water removes some of their starch.
Remove all bones from the cod before adding to the mixture; pinch the cooked cod to find and remove bones.
Keep the deep-fried balls in an uncovered dish in a 200°F oven until ready to serve.

CREAMED COD

- 1½ to 2 lb salt cod
- 3 tbsp butter
- 4 cups milk
- 1 medium onion, finely chopped
- ½ cup broth from the boiled potatoes
- 4 to 5 tbsp all-purpose flour
- ½ tsp black pepper

Soak the cod for 4 hours, changing the water twice. In a saucepan half filled with water, bring the cod to a simmer (do not boil) for 2 to 3 minutes, drain, and repeat. Flake the cod, removing any silver skin and bones.

In a large frying pan, sauté the onion in the butter until soft. Add 3 cups milk and bring to a simmer. Add the flaked cod; season with pepper to taste.

Combine the flour with the remaining 1 cup milk in a bowl or Mason jar and whisk together.

Slowly pour the flour-milk mixture into the simmering cod mixture. Stir until it reaches the desired consistency. If it appears too thick, add more milk or broth.

Serve topped with a pat of butter and with boiled potatoes.

Bonita's notes

Sprinkle the creamed cod with Colman's dry mustard for a delicious variation.

COD LOAF

- 2 cups fresh cod (2 to 3 small fillets)
- 2 cups bread crumbs
- 1 large onion, chopped
- 2 large eggs
- 1 tsp dried savoury
- 1 tsp sea salt
- ½ tsp black pepper
- ½ cup cubed fat pork (optional)
- 1 tsp olive oil
- 1 tsp butter

Place the cod in a saucepan half filled with water and ½ teaspoon salt. Bring to a simmer and cook on a low heat for 5 to 10 minutes. Remove from the pan and flake, discarding any bones and silver skin. Place the cod in a bowl.

Place the oil and butter in a frying pan set on a medium heat. Add the onions and cook until softened, then add them to the prepared cod.

Fry the fat pork cubes in the same frying pan until they are golden brown. Drain all but 1 tablespoon of rendered fat (reserve drained fat if desired for roux); add the pork cubes and remaining tablespoon of fat to the bowl, along with the bread crumbs, savoury, ½ teaspoon salt, and pepper. If not using fat pork, replace with 1 tablespoon oil.

Crack the eggs into a separate bowl, whisk lightly, and pour over the mixture. Toss until all ingredients are combined.

Line a loaf pan with parchment paper. Scoop the cod mixture into the pan and flatten down.

Bake in a preheated 350°F oven for 40 minutes to 1 hour.

Serve with boiled or baked potatoes and a roux (recipe next page) to pour on each serving.

Bonita's notes

Frying the onions and fat pork before adding them to the cod mixture helps build flavour and improve the texture.

Roux

2 tbsp butter or fat pork oil

2 tbsp all-purpose flour

pinch of sea salt

pinch of black pepper

2 cups milk of choice or half milk and half broth

1 small onion, chopped

Fry the onion with the butter until soft. Add the flour and continue cooking while stirring for a few seconds to make a paste. Add the milk and salt and pepper to taste. Whisk until thickened but still a liquid.

COD CAKES

1½ cups salt cod (about 2 small fillets, or 1 lb)

4 tbsp butter

3 tsp olive oil

1 medium onion, halved

6 medium potatoes, peeled and cut in chunks

1 large egg

2 tsp dried savoury

black pepper to taste

sea salt to taste

½ cup all-purpose flour

Soak the cod overnight, then drain. Half fill a medium saucepan with water, add the cod, and bring to a simmer. Cook for 10 to 15 minutes. Drain and flake the cod, checking for and removing all bones.

Half fill a second saucepan with water. Add ½ teaspoon salt (optional), one onion half, and the potato. Cook until the potatoes are fork-tender. Drain.

Finely chop the remaining onion. Melt 1 tablespoon butter with 1 teaspoon oil in a medium frying pan. Add the onion and fry until golden brown.

Mash the potatoes, onions, savoury, egg, and pepper in a large bowl. Add the cod and continue to mash.

Put the flour on a plate or shallow bowl. Using an ice cream scoop to measure the cod-potato mixture (about ¼ cup), form each into a flat patty, then coat it in flour. Set on a plate until all the cakes have been made.

Preheat a frying pan on a medium heat on the stovetop. Add 1 teaspoon butter and 1 teaspoon oil. Fry the cod cakes, about 4 at a time, for about 3 minutes per side or until they are golden brown.

Makes 12 medium cod cakes.

Bonita's notes

Uncooked cod cakes freeze well in a freezer bag. Be sure to write the date on the bag.
Fry the cubed fat pork with another medium chopped onion to make scruncheons to serve with the cod cakes.

COD NUGGETS

2 cod fillets (about 1 lb), skin and bones removed

Dry rub #1

½ cup all-purpose flour

pinch of sea salt and pepper

Wet wash

2 eggs

½ cup milk

pinch of sea salt and pepper

Dry rub #2

1 cup all-purpose flour

¼ cup cornmeal

½ tsp black pepper

½ tsp sea salt

½ tsp ground cumin

¼ tsp paprika

½ tsp dried thyme

½ tsp onion powder

Rinse the cod in cold water and cut in 1½-inch chunks.

Combine dry rub #1 ingredients in a bowl or bag.

Combine dry rub #2 ingredients in a bowl or bag.

Whisk together the wet wash ingredients in a small bowl.

Roll the cod pieces in dry rub #1, then in the wet wash, and then in dry rub #2. Place on a plate until all the pieces have been coated.

Preheat the deep fryer to 360°F. Fry the cod for about 5 minutes each, about 6 pieces at a time.

Keep uncovered in a 200°F oven until ready to eat. Top with vinegar and salt, and serve with tartar sauce and fries or a salad.

Bonita's notes

Leaving the cod partially frozen makes it easier to cut into chunks.
After frying, place the nuggets on a paper towel to absorb the excess oil.

COD PIE

- 2 fillets (about 1 lb) fresh or salted cod, skin and bones removed
- 6 medium potatoes, peeled
- 2 medium onions, chopped
- 2 tbsp butter
- ¼ cup milk
- 1 tbsp olive oil
- 2 tbsp all-purpose flour
- ½ tsp dried savoury
- 1 tsp black pepper
- 1½ tsp sea salt
- 1 cup vegetable broth

Boil the potatoes in a medium saucepan half filled with water, ½ teaspoon salt, and ¼ chopped onion, until fork-tender. Drain the vegetable water into a bowl, then mash the potatoes and onions with 1 tablespoon butter and the milk.

In another medium saucepan, cover the cod with water and add ¼ onion. Add ½ teaspoon salt if using fresh cod. Boil for 5 minutes. Drain and flake the cod, ensuring that all bones have been removed.

In a medium frying pan, fry the remaining onions in butter and oil, with a pinch of salt and pepper, until partially cooked. Add the flour, fry 1 minute, stirring constantly. Add the reserved vegetable water and continue cooking until thickened.

Grease a pie pan or pan of choice with butter and add half of the mashed potatoes. Lay the cod on the potatoes. Place the drawn butter and fried onions on the cod. Top with the remaining mashed potatoes.

Melt ½ teaspoon butter and brush on the mashed potatoes before baking in a preheated 350°F oven for 30 minutes or until golden brown.

Serve with fresh bread or rolls and mustard pickles or corn relish.

Bonita's notes

If using salted cod, soak in cold water overnight or double boil by boiling first in hot water, drain, then add more hot water, and boil for 5 minutes.

GRILLED COD TACOS

2 cod fillets (about 1 lb), skin and bones removed

1 tbsp olive oil

½ tsp sea salt

½ tsp black pepper

½ tsp ground cumin

½ tsp ground coriander

¼ tsp cayenne pepper

2 tbsp all-purpose flour

1 recipe Soft Taco Shells (page 128)

1 recipe Salsa (page 128)

shredded lettuce, chopped red onion, sour cream, avocado, and other toppings of choice to serve

Combine the seasonings and flour in a small plastic bag. Add the cod and toss with the seasonings to coat.

Turn the barbecue grill on high. Place the cod on a grate that has been brushed with oil, and place on the grill. Cook 3 to 4 minutes per side. When cooked through, remove from the grill and cover with aluminum foil until ready to serve.

Soft Taco Shells

2½ cups all-purpose flour, plus more for rolling

1 tsp baking powder

1½ tsp sea salt

¾ cup warm water

3 tbsp olive oil

Combine all the dry ingredients in a medium bowl. Mix in the oil and warm water until the ingredients start to come together in a ball.

Place the dough ball on the countertop or a board and knead, adding more flour if it is too sticky.

Cut the dough into 15 pieces, depending on the size of tacos preferred. Roll each piece into a ball, then roll out into a flat shell with a rolling pin.

Cook the shells on a baking sheet in a 350°F preheated oven for 10 to 15 minutes, or until golden brown. Alternatively, cook the shells in a dry frying pan or over an open flame on the grill, about 2 to 3 minutes per side. Wrap the shells in a towel to keep them warm as you go.

Salsa

3 medium tomatoes

1 bunch of cilantro, chopped

¼ hot or mild pepper

2 green onions

½ tsp ground cumin

½ tsp sea salt

Chop the tomato, peppers, and green onion in small pieces and place in a small bowl. Add the cumin, salt, and cilantro to taste. Refrigerate until ready to use, or up to 3 days.

Bonita's notes

Make the taco shells first to have them ready to serve when the cod is cooked.
Cooled taco shells can be stored in a plastic storage bag at room temperature for 2 to 3 days or frozen.

LEMON-DILL BAKED COD

- 6 cod fillets, bones and skin removed
- 2 medium onions, sliced
- 4 or 5 stems of fresh dill
- 2 or 3 lemons, sliced
- pinch of sea salt
- pinch of white pepper
- pinch of onion powder
- 2 cloves garlic, grated
- 1 cup vegetable broth
- 2 tbsp butter

Place the onions in a roasting pan or casserole dish.

Lay the cod fillets on the onions and season with the salt, pepper, garlic, dill, and lemon. Add the broth and cover with a lid or aluminum foil.

Bake in a preheated 375°F oven for 35 to 40 minutes or until fork-tender.

Serve with fresh vegetables and steamed rice.

Photo on next page

Lemon-dill baked cod

SALMON LOAF *with Dill Sauce*

1 to 2 cups chopped salmon, canned or uncooked fresh

2 medium potatoes, peeled

1 tbsp butter

1 cup bread crumbs

¼ cup evaporated milk

1 large egg

1 small onion, grated

1 stalk celery, diced

1 green onion, chopped

½ tsp sea salt

½ tsp white pepper

½ tsp onion powder

¼ cup crispy onions for garnish

Boil the potatoes until fork-tender; drain and mash with the butter.

Combine all the ingredients in a large bowl. If using fresh salmon, lightly chop and add to the mixture. For canned salmon, drain the liquid and remove any bones before adding.

Line a loaf pan with parchment paper, add the salmon mixture, and smooth the top.

Bake in a preheated 350°F oven for 40 to 45 minutes.

While waiting for the loaf to bake, make the dill sauce.

Photo on page 134

Dill Sauce

2 tbsp all-purpose flour

2 tbsp butter

1 small onion, diced

½ tsp fresh or dried dill

½ tsp sea salt

½ tsp white pepper

1 cup milk

1 cup white wine or vegetable broth

1 tbsp lemon juice

½ tsp onion powder

Fry the butter, onion, salt, pepper, and onion powder in a large frying pan on a medium heat until the onion has softened.

Add the flour and cook to a paste. Deglaze with wine or vegetable broth. Whisk until the flour mixture starts to thicken.

Add the milk, dill, and lemon juice. Continue to whisk, and lower the heat to a simmer. Add more milk or broth if the sauce becomes too thick. Adjust the seasonings to taste.

Salmon loaf with dill sauce

Turkey cabbage rolls

Entrées

The recipes I've included here are some of our favourite, tried and true meals. Some are traditional, some are modern, and a few are my own; all are created out of my love for cooking and crafting affordable meals.

BAKED BEANS

- 2 cups white pea or navy beans
- 2 medium onions, chopped
- 5 cups cold water
- 2 tsp cider vinegar, or vinegar of choice
- 1 tbsp brown sugar
- 1 tsp mustard powder
- ¼ cup molasses
- ½ cup ketchup
- pinch of black pepper
- ½ tsp sea salt
- 1 cup chopped fat pork or bacon

Place the beans in a medium stockpot with a lid and cover them with cold water. Add the salt and let the beans soak overnight.

Place the onions in a cast-iron or ceramic pot with a cover.

Drain the beans, top with fresh cold water, and boil for 1½ hours on a medium heat with the cover partially off. Drain and add to the onions. Add the cold water.

Combine the remaining ingredients, except the pork, in a small bowl. Pour over the onions and beans, mix, then top with the fat pork. Cover.

Bake in a preheated 325°F oven for 3½ to 4 hours. Check halfway through the baking time, add more water if needed, then cover and continue baking.

Bonita's notes

This recipe can be easily doubled.
Boiling the beans for 1½ hours greatly reduces the baking time.
Frying the onions or fat pork before adding to the dish gives the beans a caramelized taste.

Bonita's
Kitchen

BAKED HAM *and Scalloped Potatoes*

1 smoked picnic ham

2 medium onions:
1 chopped, 1 sliced

1 tbsp black peppercorns

1 medium onion, sliced

8 red cherries (optional)

¼ tsp black pepper

Sauce

1 cup crushed or
cubed pineapple

1 cup brown sugar

¼ cup cold water

1 tbsp cornstarch

Half fill a large stockpot with water. Add the ham, peppercorns, and chopped onion. Bring to a boil and simmer on a medium heat for 2 hours.

Carefully remove the ham from the stockpot and place it in a large bowl. Remove the net (if present) from the ham and discard. Cut the excess fat from the ham. Place the sliced onion in the bottom of a roasting pan, set the ham on the onion, and add 1 cup water.

Combine the sauce ingredients and pour over the ham. Sprinkle with the pepper and cherries, if using.

Bake, covered, in a preheated 350°F oven for 1 hour. Remove the cover and bake another 15 minutes to brown the top, if desired.

Remove the roasting pan from the oven and let the ham rest for 10 minutes. Carve as desired and serve with the pineapple sauce.

Scalloped Potatoes

4 medium potatoes, peeled and thinly sliced

3 cups shredded cheddar cheese

2 tbsp butter

1 large egg

1 cup milk

¼ cup cold water

2 tbsp all-purpose flour or cornstarch

1 tsp olive oil

sea salt and black pepper to taste

Place the potatoes in cold water until ready to use.

Place a small saucepan on a medium heat. In it, melt the butter, add the flour, and whisk until combined. Add the milk and 2 cups cheese and continue whisking to mix.

Whisk together the cold water and egg. Whisk this mixture into the saucepan to combine. Add pepper to taste and continue boiling until the sauce starts to thicken. Remove from the heat.

Pour about 1 teaspoon oil into a round glass baking dish. Add the potatoes, sauce, cheese, and salt and pepper to taste in layers. Top with remaining cheese, salt, and pepper. Bake in a preheated 350°F oven for 40 minutes, or until the potatoes are tender.

Remove from the oven and cover with aluminum foil until ready to serve.

Bonita's notes

Picnic ham often has a tough skin with a layer of fat underneath. This should be removed before baking.
Boiling the ham before baking it softens it and removes some of the fat.
Soaking the potato slices before baking removes some of the starch.

BREAKFAST MUFFINS

6 eggs

¼ cup milk or cream

12 thin slices of ham

1 cup shredded cheese of choice; more for topping

pinch of sea salt

pinch of black pepper

1 tomato, chopped

¼ cup bacon bits

½ tsp onion powder

pinch of Italian seasoning, or seasoning of choice

Crack all the eggs into a bowl and whisk together. Add all the other ingredients except the ham.

Spray a 12-cup muffin pan with oil or coat with butter. Place 1 slice of ham in each muffin cup.

Pour equal amounts of the egg mixture into each cup. Top with additional shredded cheese and a pinch of Italian seasoning.

Bake in a preheated 350°F oven for 30 minutes. Allow to cool for 5 minutes before removing from the pan.

Recipe by my husband and cameraman, Raymond Hussey.

Photos on next pages

Bonita's notes

Add any type of cooked vegetable, cheese, or meat to the egg mixture.
These can be frozen in an airtight container and gently defrosted for a quick meal.

Breakfast muffins

CORNED BEEF HASH

Version 1

1 can (340 g) corned beef

1 medium onion, chopped

375 g frozen hash browns

black pepper to taste

2 tbsp butter

1 tsp onion powder

VERSION 1

Butter a piece of parchment paper which has been placed on a baking sheet. Spread the hash browns on the parchment and bake in a preheated 350°F oven until golden brown.

Place 1 tablespoon butter, the onions, pepper, and onion powder in a frying pan and fry until the onions are light brown and cooked. Scoop the onions into a deep bowl.

Chop the corned beef into small pieces and fry in the same frying pan. Add to the onions.

Remove the hash browns from the oven and add to the corned beef. Toss.

Serve hot with warm homemade bread, ketchup, and pickles.

Version 2

1 can (340 g) corned beef

4 medium white potatoes, peeled and boiled

1 medium onion, chopped

black pepper to taste

2 tbsp butter

1 tsp onion powder

1 tbsp milk

1 tsp sea salt

VERSION 2

Mash the potatoes with 1 tablespoon butter and the milk.

Fry the onions and corned beef as in Version 1. Add to the mashed potatoes and mash everything together. Keep the corned beef hash warm in the frying pan, covered, until ready to serve.

Serve hot with pickles and fresh bread.

Bonita's notes

The hash browns can be fried instead of baked.

CREAMY MUSTARD BAKED CHICKEN

2 to 4 chicken breasts or thighs

2 tbsp Mother's Mustard Sauce (page 8)

1 package (8 oz) cream cheese

1 cup shredded cheese of choice

1 medium onion, chopped

½ bell pepper, any colour, chopped

2 cups milk

2 tbsp all-purpose flour

2 tbsp butter

½ tsp sea salt

½ tsp white pepper

1 clove garlic, pressed or grated

Parmesan cheese and green onion slices for garnish

Melt the butter in a saucepan. Sprinkle in the flour and mix until combined. Cook about 1 minute.

Whisk in the milk slowly until the sauce thickens. Add the cream cheese, mustard sauce, pepper, salt, and garlic. Continue whisking; add more milk if needed.

Place the onions and bell peppers in a large oven-safe dish. Lay the chicken in a single layer on the vegetables. Pour the sauce over the chicken and top with the cheese. Cover the pan with its lid or aluminum foil.

Bake in a preheated 350°F oven for 40 minutes. Uncover halfway through. Check before removing from the oven; a longer baking time is needed if the chicken pieces are large.

Serve with pasta or rice.

CRISPY SEASONED POTATO WEDGES AND CHICKEN

4 medium potatoes, washed, unpeeled

6 pieces of chicken (wings, legs, or thighs are preferred), skin on

Wet mixture
1 cup milk

1 large egg

½ tsp sea salt

Dry mixture
3 cups flour of choice

2 tsp sea salt

2 tsp ground cumin

1 tsp cayenne pepper

1½ tsp black pepper

1½ tsp ground thyme

1½ tsp garlic powder

1½ tsp onion powder

1½ tsp paprika

>>

Cut the potatoes into 6 to 8 wedges. Place them in a bowl of water to remove some of the starch.

Combine the wet mixture ingredients in a separate bowl.

Combine the dry mixture ingredients in a third bowl.

Put 1 cup of the dry mixture at a time into a plastic bag. Toss 2 or 3 potato wedges at a time through the wet mixture and then in the dry mixture. Continue until all the wedges are coated, then repeat with a second coating of wet then dry mixture. After all the potato wedges have been coated, follow the same method for the chicken pieces.

Heat the deep fryer to 375°F. Fry 4 or 5 potato wedges at a time until golden brown, about 5 to 7 minutes; remove them and drain on a paper towel. Keep warm in a 200°F oven, uncovered, until ready to serve.

Deep-fry the chicken until golden brown and cooked to 165°F, about 7 to 10 minutes.

▶▶

<<

◀◀

Onion dip
1 tbsp onion soup mix

1 tbsp sour cream

3 tbsp mayonnaise

1 tbsp olive oil

1 green onion, chopped

Quick gravy
1 tbsp onion soup mix

2 tbsp cornstarch

2 tbsp Oxo or Bovril

1 cup hot water

ONION DIP

Combine the sour cream, mayonnaise, and onion soup mix. Top with the green onions.

QUICK GRAVY

Combine all the gravy ingredients and mix well. Microwave for 30 seconds to 1 minute or until the mixture has thickened.

Bonita's notes

Small pieces of chicken, such as wings, legs, and thighs, cook faster than larger pieces. If using larger pieces, adjust the frying time accordingly.

DUCHESS POTATOES

- 6 large potatoes, peeled and quartered
- ¼ cup melted butter, extra for brushing
- ¼ cup evaporated milk or cream
- 1 tsp sea salt
- ½ tsp black pepper
- 2 egg yolks
- ½ tsp dried parsley
- 1 clove garlic, pressed or chopped
- ½ cup Parmesan cheese

Boil the potatoes with ½ teaspoon salt in a medium saucepan half filled with water until they are fork-tender.

Drain the potatoes. Mash the potatoes with the butter and garlic.

Whisk together the milk and egg yolks. Add to the mashed potatoes and combine. Add the Parmesan cheese, ½ teaspoon salt, and pepper. Mix until thick and creamy.

Line a baking sheet with parchment paper. Spoon the potatoes into a large piping bag with a large star tip.

Pipe 1½-inch-diameter piles (about the size of a small egg) of mashed potatoes about ½ inch apart.

Brush the tops of the potatoes with additional butter.

Bake in a preheated 375°F oven for 20 minutes or until golden brown.

Bonita's notes

These can be made in advance and rewarmed. They also freeze well after they have been baked and cooled. These are delicious served with gravy or topped with more Parmesan cheese.

HAM QUICHE

1 cup cubed ham

2 cups prepared hash browns, frozen or thawed

5 large eggs

¼ cup evaporated milk

½ small onion, chopped

½ green pepper, chopped

½ stalk celery, chopped

1 green onion, chopped

½ tsp onion powder

½ tsp sea salt

½ tsp white pepper

1 tbsp melted butter

Whisk together the eggs, milk, and seasonings. Add the ham, onion, celery, green pepper, and green onion and fold together.

Spread the hash browns on the bottom and sides of a pie pan or quiche dish. Pour the butter over the hash browns. Add the egg mixture.

Bake in a preheated 350°F oven for 45 minutes or until the eggs are set.

Serve topped with sour cream, salsa, additional green onion, and shredded cheese.

Bonita's notes

To speed up the prep time, peel and cut all the vegetables beforehand. Refrigerate in a container with a lid. This can be cooked in a slow cooker as well: layer the ingredients as above, set on low, and cook 4 to 6 hours.

LEMON AND HERB CHICKEN

1 chicken, cut in pieces

2 tbsp olive oil

2 tbsp lemon juice

½ tsp dried or 1 tbsp fresh rosemary

½ tsp dried sage

½ tsp mustard powder

⅛ tsp cayenne pepper

½ tsp white pepper

2 tbsp all-purpose flour

2 cups chicken broth

½ tsp sea salt

2 tbsp butter

½ tsp onion powder

1 medium onion, chopped

1 green onion, chopped

1 lemon, sliced

Place the chicken pieces in a bowl or plastic bag. Drizzle with the oil and season with the rosemary, sage, onion powder, ¼ teaspoon salt, cayenne pepper, and ¼ teaspoon pepper. Toss until the seasonings are evenly spread over the chicken.

Place a large frying pan on a medium heat. When the pan is heated, add the chicken and brown on both sides; this will take about 10 minutes.

Melt the butter in a second frying pan on a medium heat and add the chopped onion; fry until partly cooked. Add the flour and the remainder of the salt and pepper. Stir continuously until the flour and onion are cooked and the roux is thick, about 2 or 3 minutes.

Gradually add the broth, mustard, and lemon juice. Keep stirring until the roux is smooth and creamy; add more broth if needed.

Transfer the roux to the frying pan with the chicken and stir to coat. Cover and cook on a low to medium heat for 30 to 40 minutes. Alternatively, bake the chicken in a preheated 350°F oven for 30 minutes.

Place the chicken on a serving platter. Top with the lemon slices and green onion.

Bonita's notes

Frying the chicken before baking it locks in the juice and builds flavour.

PORK CHOP DINNER

4 pork chops, any cut

1 medium onion, sliced

1 small turnip, peeled and cubed

2 large potatoes, peeled and cubed

2 large carrots, peeled and cubed

3 tbsp butter, melted

2 cups bread crumbs, seasoned to taste

1 tsp sea salt

½ tsp black pepper

½ cup vegetable or chicken broth

¼ tsp ground nutmeg

½ tsp brown sugar

2 apples, peeled and cut in wedges

¼ cup (or more) of green beans, cut or full

Place 2 tablespoons melted butter in a roasting pan. Add the prepared vegetables and toss to coat. Sprinkle with the salt and pepper, cover, and bake in a preheated 425°F oven for 20 minutes.

Trim the fat from the pork chops and sprinkle both sides with bread crumbs. After the vegetables have cooked for 20 minutes, place the coated pork chops in a single layer on the vegetables. Bake, uncovered, for 35 to 40 minutes or until the pork is cooked through. Check the pan halfway through the baking time to ensure that the vegetables are not burning; add more broth if needed.

Meanwhile, place the prepared apples and 1 tablespoon butter in a large saucepan on a medium heat. Add the nutmeg and brown sugar and fry for 4 or 5 minutes. Add the green beans, sprinkle with salt, and cook until the beans are tender.

Remove the pork chops from the oven and serve with the apples and beans.

Bonita's notes

The vegetables can be fried instead of baked; if so, add them to the roasting pan and top with the pork chops. Peeling the apples before frying is optional.

Rolled mushroom meatloaf

ROLLED MUSHROOM MEATLOAF

1 lb lean ground beef

1 can (284 ml) sliced mushrooms or 2 cups sliced fresh mushrooms

1 large onion, chopped

1 tsp black pepper

1 tsp sea salt

1 tsp onion powder

1 tbsp butter

1 tsp olive oil

Combine the beef with ½ teaspoon of each seasoning.

Place a piece of parchment paper on the countertop and scoop the seasoned beef on it. Place another piece of parchment paper on the beef and roll it out with a rolling pin.

Fry the onions, butter, oil, pepper, and salt in a frying pan on a medium heat. Add the mushrooms. Continue frying until the onions are golden brown. Allow the mushrooms and onions to cool to room temperature before placing them on the rolled beef.

Remove the top piece of parchment paper from the beef. Spoon the fried onions and mushrooms on the beef and spread out evenly. Starting from the nearest end, use the parchment paper to roll the beef outward into a loaf.

Use the parchment paper to lift the rolled meatloaf into a loaf pan. Leave the parchment paper in place to help remove the cooked loaf from the pan but trim any overhanging paper.

Sprinkle the remaining seasonings on the meatloaf. Bake in a preheated 350°F oven for 60 minutes or until it is cooked through. Allow the meatloaf to rest for 5 minutes before removing it from the pan.

Cut in slices and serve with gravy, pasta sauce, or sauce of choice.

Photos on previous pages

Bonita's notes

After opening the package of ground beef, rinse the beef with cold water to remove any blood.

STUFFED PORK TENDERLOIN ROAST

2 lb pork loin roast, larger if desired

3 cups bread crumbs

1 tsp dried savoury

1 tsp sea salt

1 tsp black pepper

2 tbsp melted butter

2 large carrots, chopped

1 medium onion, chopped

2 medium potatoes, chopped

1 tsp onion powder

½ small turnip, chopped

2 strips of bacon

2 tbsp all-purpose flour

3 cups vegetable or chicken broth

To make the stuffing: Mix the bread crumbs, savoury, a pinch of salt and pepper, and 1 tablespoon melted butter by hand, pinching the butter into the crumbs. Add half the chopped onion and continue mixing through.

With the pork roast on a cutting board, place your hand on the top of the roast and slowly and carefully use a sharp knife to make a cut into the side of the roast, about 1 inch deep. Start cutting through the roast. Keep rolling the roast as you cut *but don't* cut through—the goal is to cut the roast until it is flat. If you are unfamiliar with this technique, watch the video at BonitasKitchen.com/recipe/stuffed-pork-tenderloin-roast/.

Scoop the stuffing onto the flattened pork roast and roll up, starting at the nearest end.

Tie a piece of cotton string around the pork to hold it together. Wrap the bacon around the rolled pork and season with salt, pepper, and onion powder.

▶▶

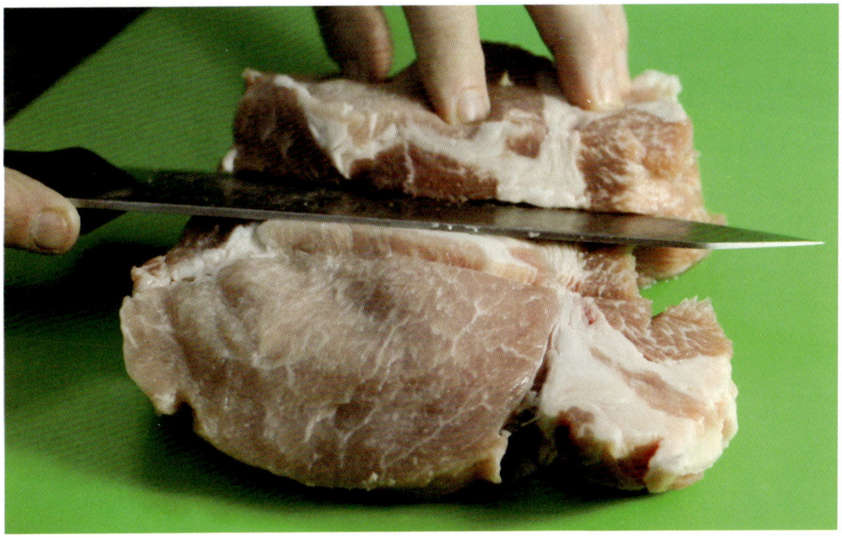

Place the pork in a roasting pan, and add the rest of the onion and other vegetables to the pan around the roast. Add the broth. Roast in a preheated 400°F oven uncovered for 45 minutes to 1 hour. Check the roast halfway through the baking time, basting with pan drippings.

When the pork has cooked through, remove it from the oven and let it rest while making gravy from the drippings. Melt 1 tablespoon butter in a frying pan on a medium heat. Add the flour and mix until it is cooked. Slowly add the drippings and the broth, stirring until the gravy starts to thicken. Adjust the seasonings to taste.

Slice the pork and serve with the pan vegetables and gravy.

Bonita's notes

Keep stale bread or bread heels in the freezer in a freezer bag to use for stuffings. Chop or grate the onion, the latter if more liquid and a faster cooking time are desired.

STUFFED MEATBALLS

1 lb lean ground beef

1 medium onion, grated

12 yellow pearl onions

12 baby potatoes

2 cloves garlic, pressed

1 large egg

1 tsp black pepper

1 tsp sea salt

1 tsp onion powder

1 cup bread crumbs

Italian seasoning to taste

½ tbsp Parmesan cheese

Combine the beef, grated onion, garlic, ½ teaspoon pepper, ½ teaspoon salt, ½ teaspoon onion powder, egg, and ½ cup bread crumbs. Fold together by hand or with a spoon until all the ingredients have been equally mixed but not over-mixed.

Wash the potatoes, leaving the skins on. Wrap about 2 tablespoons of the beef mixture around 1 potato or 1 onion and place on a plate. Continue with the rest of the beef mixture.

Toss ½ cup bread crumbs with ½ teaspoon salt, ½ teaspoon pepper, ½ teaspoon onion powder, Italian seasoning, and Parmesan cheese.

Roll each meatball in the bread crumbs and place on a baking sheet which has been lined with parchment paper.

Bake in a preheated 375°F oven for 30 to 45 minutes, turning halfway to brown both sides.

Serve with pasta sauce or gravy, or use the meatballs in a sub.

Bonita's notes

If lean ground beef is not available, use medium ground and place a rack on the baking sheet so that the oil drips away from the meatballs.

TANGY MUSTARD PORK CHOPS

4 pork chops, any cut

1 medium onion, sliced

1 medium bell pepper, any colour, sliced

1 cup Mother's Mustard Sauce (page 8)

1 apple, cut in wedges

2 tbsp olive oil

pinch of sea salt

pinch of black pepper

pinch of onion powder

1 tbsp all-purpose flour

2 cups vegetable or beef broth

Pour 1 tablespoon oil into a cast-iron or oven-proof pan and bring to a medium heat.

Season the pork chops with the salt, pepper, and onion powder on both sides. Spread 1 teaspoon of the mustard sauce on both sides of the chops. Add the chops to the hot frying pan and fry for 3 or 4 minutes on each side. Add the onions, peppers, and apple and fry for another 4 minutes.

Bake in a preheated 350°F oven, uncovered, for 20 to 25 minutes, depending on the size and thickness of the chops.

When the chops have cooked through, place them on a plate. Place the frying pan on a medium heat. Add 1 tablespoon oil, the flour, and broth to deglaze the pan; whisk into a smooth gravy.

Serve with vegetables or steamed rice and topped with gravy.

STUFFED ZUCCHINI

- 2 large zucchini (12 inches or longer)
- 2 lb lean ground beef or chicken
- 1 large onion, chopped
- 2 cups shredded cheddar cheese
- 1 tsp onion powder
- 1 tsp garlic powder
- 2 tbsp olive oil
- 1 tsp sea salt
- 1 tsp black pepper
- 2 tbsp all-purpose flour
- 2 tbsp butter
- 1 cup broth of choice
- 1 cup milk

Cut the zucchini in half longitudinally. Scoop out the flesh, leaving the skin intact. Chop the flesh into small pieces.

Pour the oil into a large frying pan and start to fry the ground beef on a medium heat. When it is partially cooked, add the zucchini and onion. Add the pepper, salt, onion powder, and garlic powder. Fry until the beef is cooked and the zucchini has softened. Remove the pan from the heat and scoop the beef-zucchini mixture into a bowl. Return the pan to the stovetop.

Add the butter and olive oil to the frying pan. When the butter has melted, add the flour and mix well. Add the broth and milk and continue mixing until the liquid starts to thicken. Add 1 cup cheese and continue mixing for a few seconds.

Return the beef mixture to the frying pan and toss with the sauce. Scoop the mixture into the zucchini shells and top with the remaining cheese. Season to taste.

Bake in a preheated 350°F oven for 45 to 60 minutes.

TURKEY CABBAGE ROLLS

- 1 lb ground turkey
- 2 cups rice of choice, uncooked
- 1 medium onion, chopped
- 1 medium carrot, peeled and grated
- 1 bottle (600 ml) pasta sauce of choice
- 1 large green cabbage
- 1 tsp sea salt
- ½ tsp black pepper
- ½ tsp onion powder
- ½ tsp garlic powder or 1 clove garlic, pressed

Bring a large saucepan half filled with water to a boil. Add ½ teaspoon salt and the cabbage. Partially cook. Remove the cabbage from the water and cut off the leaves one at a time and place them on a plate (13 to 15 leaves are required for this recipe).

Combine the turkey, rice, carrot, chopped onion, pepper, ½ teaspoon salt, onion powder, and garlic powder in a medium bowl.

Pour the pasta sauce into a separate bowl and add 1 bottle of water (rinse the bottle and pour into the bowl). Add 1½ cups of this liquid to the turkey.

▶▶

Bonita's notes

Always place a slow cooker on a safe surface. The cabbage rolls can be prepared and refrigerated overnight before being cooked.

◀◀

Grate 1 cup of the remaining partially cooked cabbage. Add to the turkey and stir together.

The cabbage rolls may be cooked in a slow cooker or a roasting pan with a lid (or use aluminum foil).

Line the bottom of a slow cooker or roasting pan with 2 cabbage leaves.

Lay a cabbage leaf on the counter or a cutting board. Scoop about ⅓ cup of the turkey mixture onto the leaf. Roll outward, pulling in the sides of the leaf while rolling to make a tight package. Continue with the rest of the turkey mixture.

Place the rolls in the slow cooker, making two layers. Place the top layer at right angles to the bottom layer.

Pour the remainder of the thinned pasta sauce on the cabbage rolls. Cook on low for 8 to 10 hours or on high for 4 to 6 hours. Alternatively, bake in a preheated 350°F for 60 minutes, covered. Baste with the pasta sauce and add more liquid if needed. Re-cover and bake for another 60 minutes. Turn off the heat and let rest 10 minutes in the oven before serving.

Photo on page 136

TURKEY DINNER FOR TWO

For the turkey and dressing
1 or 2 turkey breasts

2 cups bread crumbs

1 tbsp dried savoury

2 tbsp butter

1 medium onion, chopped

1 cup turkey or chicken broth

¼ cup dried cranberries

1 apple, peeled and cubed

1 tsp sea salt

1 tsp black pepper

1 tsp onion powder

>>

Debone the turkey breast (leave the skin on) and cut through the centre to allow the breast to open flat on a plate. Set aside until ready to use.

Combine the bread crumbs, savoury, ½ teaspoon salt, ½ teaspoon pepper, ½ teaspoon onion powder, 1 tablespoon chopped onion, cranberries, and apple. Melt 1 tablespoon butter and add. Pinch the stuffing ingredients together by hand.

Place 1 cup or more of the stuffing mixture on each flattened turkey breast and pat down. Roll the breast up outward and tie with cotton string.

Place the remainder of the chopped onion and 1 cup broth in a roasting pan with a lid. Place the rolled turkey breasts on the onion. Insert small slivers of butter under the skin. Sprinkle with the remaining pepper, salt, and onion powder.

Bake in a preheated 400°F oven for 60 minutes or until cooked through. Let the turkey breasts rest for 15 minutes before slicing them. Reserve drippings.

For the sides: Bring a saucepan half filled with water to a boil. Add 1 teaspoon sea salt, the onion, and prepared potatoes, carrots, and turnips. Boil on a medium heat until fork-tender. Drain, reserving the water.

▶▶

<<

For the sides

4 medium potatoes, peeled and chopped

1 small turnip, peeled and cubed

1 tbsp cream

2 tbsp butter

2 medium carrots, peeled and sliced

1 tsp sea salt

1 tsp brown sugar

green beans or peas as desired

1 small onion

For the gravy

2 tbsp butter

2 tbsp all-purpose flour

turkey gravy mix

Prepare gravy: Melt 2 tablespoons butter and 2 tablespoons flour in a small saucepan and mix together. Add the turkey drippings, vegetable water, and gravy mix. Whisk together until the gravy is thickened and smooth.

Mash the cooked potatoes with cream and 1 tablespoon butter. In another bowl, mash the carrot and turnip with 1 tablespoon butter, ½ teaspoon pepper, and 1 teaspoon brown sugar.

Steam the green beans or peas for a few minutes before serving.

Serve the turkey with the prepared vegetables and topped with gravy.

TURKEY, STUFFING, AND SAUSAGE

1 turkey

2 lb pork sausage

2 to 3 cups bread crumbs

1 medium onion, chopped

3 tbsp butter or olive oil

1 tbsp dried savoury

sea salt and black pepper to taste

Rinse the turkey in cold water; dry its interior and exterior with a paper towel. Place the turkey in a roasting pan.

Preheat the oven to 350°F. To make the stuffing: Combine the bread crumbs and butter in a bowl. Add half of the chopped onion, savoury, salt, and pepper and mix by hand.

Pack the stuffing into the turkey cavity. Stuff the neck cavity with the pork sausage: cut open the casing and squeeze the sausage into the cavity. Cover with the extra turkey skin and secure.

▶▶

◀◀

Pour 2 cups water or broth into the roasting pan. Add a pinch of salt and pepper and half of the chopped onion.

Bake the turkey for 1 hour, uncovered. Baste, cover, and bake another 90 minutes or until it is golden brown or reading 180°F on a meat thermometer. Check every 30 minutes and baste with the pan drippings.

When the turkey is cooked, remove it from the roasting pan and place it on a platter. Remove the stuffing and sausage from the cavities; cover the turkey with aluminum foil until ready to carve.

Put the roasting pan on the stovetop to make the gravy.

Gravy from turkey drippings

turkey drippings

3 cups stock or vegetable water (page 74)

1 tbsp gravy browning (optional)

¼ cup all-purpose flour or cornstarch

1 cup cold water

Mix the turkey drippings, stock or vegetable water, and gravy browning together in the roasting pan and let it come to a boil. Combine, in a Mason jar with a cover, the flour and the cold water. Shake well until smooth. When the stock has come to a boil, mix in the flour mixture until the stock starts to thicken.

Bonita's notes

The cooking time for turkey is approximately 20 minutes per pound at 350°F, or until a meat thermometer reads between 165°F and 180°F.

TURKEY PATTIES

- 2 cups chopped cooked turkey
- 5 potatoes, peeled and chopped
- 2 small onions: 1 whole, 1 grated
- sea salt and black pepper to taste
- 1 tbsp dried savoury
- 2 tbsp butter, melted
- ¼ cup cream
- 2 cups bread crumbs
- ¼ cup all-purpose flour
- butter or oil as needed

Boil the potatoes and whole onion in a medium saucepan half filled with water and a pinch of salt. Cook until tender. Drain and mash the potatoes and onion with 1 tablespoon butter, cream, and a pinch of salt and pepper.

Place bread crumbs into a medium bowl and add 1 tablespoon melted butter, 1 tablespoon savoury, the grated onion, and a pinch of salt and pepper.

Mix all the ingredients together to make a stuffing; set aside until ready to use.

Add the chopped turkey to the mashed potatoes and combine. Wrap about ¼ cup of the turkey-potato mixture around 2 tablespoons of stuffing; form into a ball and then flatten the ball into a patty.

Place the flour on a small plate or shallow bowl and season with salt and pepper to taste. Coat the patties in the flour mixture.

Fry the patties in butter or oil on a medium heat until golden brown on each side.

Bonita's notes

This is a perfect way to use up some cooked leftover turkey.

ZESTY ORANGE PORK CHOPS

2 or more lean pork chops

1 medium onion, sliced

¼ cup white wine for deglazing the pan

Marinating sauce

½ cup water

½ cup orange juice

¼ cup lemon juice

¼ cup orange marmalade

2 tbsp brown sugar

2 tbsp mustard, any type

1 tbsp orange zest

1 tbsp soy sauce

1 tbsp Worcestershire sauce

1 tsp ground ginger

1 or 2 cloves garlic, pressed

6 navel orange slices for garnish

Place the pork chops in a glass dish (do not use a metal pan for marinating).

Combine all marinating ingredients in a saucepan on a medium heat. Bring to a boil, stirring often. Remove from the heat and allow to come to room temperature, then pour the marinating sauce over the pork chops. Cover and refrigerate for 8 hours or overnight. Turn the pork chops occasionally.

Drain the marinade into a bowl and preheat the indoor grill pan or cast-iron frying pan. Grill the chops 8 to 10 minutes on each side, turning only once, until they are cooked through. Baste the chops with the marinade while grilling.

Deglaze indoor grill with the remainder of the marinade, or pour into a saucepan and bring to a boil for 5 minutes (to kill any bacteria from the raw pork), then serve with the pork chops.

Grill the orange slices just to warm them through, then place them on the pork chops.

Fry the onion slices until golden brown; serve with the pork chops.

Bonita's notes

Here's a link to our homemade marmalade! Use it in this recipe, or replace with your favourite store-bought version: *https://www.bonitaskitchen.com/recipe/orange-marmalade/*

Photo by Laura Hussey

About Bonita's Kitchen

Bonita's Kitchen started when Bonita's son asked her to share her Homemade Bread recipe on YouTube so that he could watch it anytime. Little did she know that more than just her two sons would be tuning in.

Bonita Hussey hails from the small community of Upper Island Cove, Newfoundland and Labrador, often called "the walled city." For 27 years, Bonita and her husband, Raymond, lived in Yellowknife, Northwest Territories, where they raised their two boys, Bradley and Steven.

Now retired, Bonita and Raymond spend their days FaceTiming with their grandchildren, filming episodes for Bonita's Kitchen, and soaking in the beautiful sights and sounds of Newfoundland and Labrador. They often find themselves asking, "Where did we ever find the time to work?"

Bonita and Raymond Hussey.

Artwork by Brad Hussey